E243 Inclusive Education: Learning from each other

Working it Out

BOOK 4

This book forms part of The Open University course **E243 Inclusive Education: learning from each other**. The complete list of books and units is as follows:

Readers

Nind, M., Rix, J., Sheehy, K. and Simmons, K. (eds) (2003) *Inclusive Education: diverse perspectives*, London, David Fulton in association with The Open University (**Reader 1**).

Nind, M., Sheehy, K. and Simmons, K. (eds) (2003) *Inclusive Education: learners and learning contexts*, London, David Fulton in association with The Open University (**Reader 2**).

Working it out

BOOK 4   Units 9 — 12

Education and Language Studies
Level 2

This publication forms part of an Open University course **E243 Inclusive Education: learning from each other**. Details of this and other Open University courses can be obtained from the Course Information and Advice Centre, PO Box 724, The Open University, Milton Keynes MK7 6ZS, United Kingdom: tel. +44 (0)1908 653231, e-mail general-enquiries@open.ac.uk

Alternatively, you may visit the Open University website at http://www.open.ac.uk where you can learn more about the wide range of courses and packs offered at all levels by The Open University.

To purchase a selection of Open University course materials visit the webshop at http://www.ouw.co.uk, or contact Open University Worldwide, Michael Young Building, Walton Hall, Milton Keynes MK7 6AA, United Kingdom for a brochure. tel. +44 (0)1908 858785; fax +44 (0)1908 858787; e-mail ouwenq@open.ac.uk

The Open University
Walton Hall, Milton Keynes
MK7 6AA

First published 2004

Edited, designed and typeset by The Open University.

Printed and bound in the United Kingdom by the Alden Group, Oxford.

ISBN 0 7492 5307 X

1.1

Contents

Course team

Melanie Nind	*Joint chair and author*
Kieron Sheehy	*Joint chair and author*
Katy Simmons	*Author*
Jonathan Rix	*Author*
Mary Kellett	*Author*
Caroline Roaf	*Author*
Julie Allan	*External assessor*
Brenda Jarvis	*Course manager*
Liz Santucci	*Course secretary*
Alison Goslin	*Designer*
Sian Lewis	*Designer*
Isabel Ford	*Editor*
Fiona Carey	*Editor*
Chris Gravell	*Editor*
Nicola Tolcher	*Compositor*
Deana Plummer	*Picture researcher*
Demarisse Stanley	*Rights assistant*
Michael Peet	*BBC producer*
Ian Black	*BBC researcher*
Richard Fisher	*BBC Video editor*
Steve Hoy	*BBC Sound dubbing*
John Berry	*Critical reader*
John Swain	*Critical reader*
Sally French	*Critical reader*
Helen Murphy	*Critical reader*
Jim Towers	*Critical reader*
Ronnie Flynn	*Critical reader*

Introduction

In the following units we turn our attention to diverse learners and learning contexts. In Unit 9 we are concerned with learners in the context of their local communities. We look at approaches to inclusive education that actively seek to involve the community and to address community issues. In contrast, in Unit 10 we look at learners taken out of their immediate local communities to be supported in units and resourced schools. This may mean pupils who have been excluded gain access to mainstream experiences, but not necessarily a place in a local school. In both units we look at learning environments in transition as they make adjustments to become more inclusive. The communities of learners discussed in each vary from the widest notion of inclusion groups in Unit 9 to more traditional special school populations in Unit 10.

Units 11 and 12 stand very much as a pair. We are concerned here with learners who are often at the margins of educational life because of the crises they experience and challenges they present in educational contexts that are not responsive to all learners. In Unit 11 we address the proactive/preventative work that is being done to create more inclusive environments, and in Unit 12 we look more at the reactive/crisis measures designed to maintain some links with education for pupils who are otherwise marginalized or excluded. We illustrate the important relationship between work done to promote inclusion and work done in response to possible exclusion.

UNIT 9   Learning to change

Prepared for the course team by Katy Simmons and Melanie Nind

Contents

1 Introduction

In earlier units, we have seen that inclusive practice requires us to recognize, respect and value the diverse perspectives that learners bring with them to their learning contexts. It also requires the participation of the learners themselves, so that the educational experiences offered to them change in order to acknowledge and include the diversity of learners' experiences and heritage. Such changes often require shifts both in power and in the relationships between those who teach and those who learn.

Roger Slee has argued that 'engagement and the representation of student identities are critical to an inclusive education' (Slee, 1999, p. 199). In other words, learners need to be personally engaged and able to recognize themselves and their own values, not only in what they are learning but also in the place where that learning is happening. Thinking about inclusion involves asking questions about how places of learning are organized, what is being learned, whose experiences are seen as being the most valuable and who makes decisions about what is learned.

In the units you have read so far, we have tried to look at some of these questions. Many of the questions focus on the value that schools and other organizations place on individuals or groups of learners. They also focus on how far the participation of different groups of learners is welcomed. They are questions about what is taught and to whom, and about how far learners can be different but equal.

Roger Slee's article focuses on disabled students but the questions he raises could equally well apply to any group that might be seen as marginalized. These are some of the questions which Roger Slee raises and that we are asking throughout this course:

- Where are the voices of disabled people, Travellers, women, and people from minority ethnic heritage – or any other potentially marginalized group – in the policy-making process?

- What value do we attribute to different identities, for example parent, pupil, professional, those from minority ethnic heritage, and those from marginalized groups?

- How are diverse perspectives reflected in the culture of the school, in terms of what it teaches, how it teaches and how the school is organized?

These questions are ones that concern values. Put simply, they are questions about how far learners who are seen as different are able to contribute not only to what is learned but also to the ways in which schools are organized.

We have actively sought examples of good practice, for we know through the experiences of writers such as Micheline Mason, a disabled writer and activist, what can happen when individuals or groups are not valued:

> When the Save the Children Fund did research into the attitudes of black and white children they were shocked to find that by the age of three, black children were already wanting to be white, and that both groups of children valued their white friends more than their black friends. This is the phenomenon of 'internalised oppression' – seeing that one group of people are valued more highly than another, and wanting to become like them. This happens every bit as much for disabled children and children with learning difficulties as for black children or working class children.
>
> *(Mason, 1992, p. 27)*

Roger Slee (1999) acknowledges that such questions 'travel beyond schooling in the UK' (p. 200) and holds out as a goal 'a pedagogy of recognition' (p. 200), where the curriculum is one in which diverse learners can recognize their own experiences and identities. You may have had an experience yourself (maybe even on this course) of a situation where you felt alienated from or untouched by the material you were studying. Alternatively, you may have had a learning experience where your own experience was reflected in what you were learning and where you thought 'That's about me.' Experiences in the last category can be energizing and lead to real learning.

In this unit, we shall be travelling beyond schooling, as proposed by Roger Slee, and exploring the ways in which the development of inclusive practice has, in some settings, broken down traditional barriers between classroom and community, and between users and providers of services and the professionals who staff those services. We will look at how the breaking down of these barriers can enable those who may be on the margins to participate in educational settings. We will be looking at video material that focuses on two very different settings, one in Corby, Northamptonshire, and one in Bannockburn, Scotland. In both these settings, there has been innovative and ground breaking work done to create inclusive learning environments that go beyond school. As you work through the unit, you will need to consider how far, in each setting, progress has been made towards providing learning environments where diverse groups recognize themselves and find their experiences valued.

Learning outcomes

By the end of this unit you will be able to:

- understand how emerging ideas of inclusion have affected the organization and structure of some schools and local education authorities (LEAs);

- evaluate how far particular structures encourage participation by diverse individuals and communities;
- compare practices in a range of different settings;
- discuss how changing structures and practices can create new relationships between users and providers of services.

Resources for this unit

To complete the activities in this unit you will need to have access to Reader 2 and Video Band B, and to friends or colleagues with whom you can discuss ideas. You will also need to set aside some time for reflection.

As part of your study for this unit we will ask you to read the following chapter:

- Chapter 21, 'Bridges to literacy' by Eve Gregory, in Reader 2.

For Activity 9.3 you will need to watch Video Band B, *Learning Together,* Part 1. For Activity 9.6 you will need to watch Part 2.

2 Recognizing ourselves

Learning different things

A number of writers have described their failure to recognize themselves during their time at school and the damaging effects of this lack of self-recognition. Richard Rieser, who contracted polio as a baby, describes his time as a teenager, trying to participate in a macho culture:

> The need to be tough, to cope, to be what is now called a super-cripple left no space for sensitive feelings and 'soft' creativity. These feelings of mine were much reinforced by my avid attendance at cubs and boy scout activities. The competitive, physical, cruel, jingoistic attitude that prevailed in the scouts was just what I needed to forget who I was. I threw myself into scouting, gaining all sorts of proficiency badges and eventually becoming the youngest Queen's Scout at 15. I put a brave face on things I found incredibly difficult or impossible. In one way they treated me as if I was just the same as all the others and I suppose that was why I liked it. The problem was I wasn't just the same!
>
> ... On one occasion I was pegged to the ground with wet grass and slops smeared all over me and left in the hot sun for several hours.

This was because I could not peel the potatoes well with a knife, a task I found too difficult due to my polio arm.

This ritual was supposed to make a man of you, but it just made me and the others hard, uncaring and insensitive ... I was unable to feel the strength of character I later found from being open to my feelings and so being conscious of my disability and my limitations, which also led me to try to be more sensitive and empathetic to others.

(Rieser, 1992, p. 31)

Richard Rieser did not recognize himself in the experiences that were on offer to him as a young man. In addition, his own identity and experience as a disabled person was not valued or acknowledged by others. This lack of recognition, at both internal and external levels, led him to develop a persona that was at odds with what he knew about himself.

Gwynedd Lloyd and Claire Norris, writing about the experiences of Gypsy Traveller children within the Scottish school system, show how this lack of recognition can result in marginalization and exclusion. One of their interviewees, a young woman, commented:

Travelling people learn their own different things but when you're at school you learn different things altogether ... when I grow up I just want to be here wi' my mither and that, and my brothers.

(Lloyd and Norris, 1998, p. 367)

The experience of school did not fit this young woman's experience or aspirations.

Activity 9.1   Recognizing ourselves

In your learning journal, jot down any experiences you have had where you felt 'at odds', personally or culturally, with a learning context you were involved in or an aspect of what you were trying to learn. You may have experienced this during this course, for example, when you met experiences, ideas or viewpoints that you could not share. How did this affect your learning? Also reflect on occasions where you experienced a sense of identification with your learning context and the things you were learning. In the context of this course, you may have encountered occasions where you suddenly felt 'This is about me' as you were reading. Again, how did that experience affect your learning?

You may have noted, as you worked through the activity, that the moments when you felt you learned most were those where you felt your own experience was valued. The link between personal experience and new learning is a key element of inclusive practice.

Building bridges

The link made by young children between what they already know and what they learn in school has been a focus of Eve Gregory's work. She has worked extensively with families in East London on the development of early literacy. She has written about Bangladeshi families who, though possessing a rich and varied culture of their own, do not share the 'cultural capital' of the prevailing culture and as such may be marginalized in school (Gregory and Williams, 2000). Nina, a young woman born in Spitalfields, London, whose parents came from Sylhet, describes early literacy acquisition in her family:

> I didn't have much support at home with reading because my parents couldn't ... well, they could read the basics but they wouldn't have been able to read us long stories. But they did know the basics of the alphabet and simple words but they couldn't read us English stories ... they weren't so confident in reading English and they wouldn't have been able to express their feelings in English. But they would tell us Bengali stories instead. Not when we were going to sleep, but just before we did – in a group, not every night if we were doing other things – we were quite a large family, there were five of us there. But they did a good job on bringing us up.
>
> *(Gregory and Williams, 2000, p. 124)*

In her chapter in Reader 2, Eve Gregory writes about the way in which the wealth of literacy traditions in Bangladeshi families is often unacknowledged once children start school (Reader 2, p. 265). Eve Gregory's chapter focuses on the gap between the cultural expectations reflected in official education reports and the actual practices in families whose cultural norms are different from those of education professionals.

◯ Activity 9.2 Recognizing difference

Now read the following chapter:

● Chapter 21, 'Bridges to literacy', by Eve Gregory, in Reader 2.

As you read, make a list showing the different ways that children from differing cultural groups learn to read. What implications do these differences have for young children starting school? How can schools become 'bridges' between different cultures?

Eve Gregory shows how the child-centred but adult-led model of early reading acquisition in the UK, exemplified in the reading of bedtime stories to children by their parents, does not reflect the experiences of many cultural groups. For 'English monocultural' children, she argues, literacy learning is likely to have been informal and child-centred, with the child choosing comics or computer games, sometimes supported by an adult. A Bangladeshi child, in contrast, is likely to have had experience of learning the Qur'an in formal groups, using repetition, practice and testing. Literacy acquisition is likely to have been seen as a serious rather than fun activity and to have been based on school books.

Eve Gregory details the richness of the experience that children from diverse cultural backgrounds are likely to have had, ranging from formal experiences of Qur'anic and Bengali classes to more informal reading with siblings and family at home. However, she suggests these experiences often do not count in terms of the models promoted in schools. Their difference in styles of literacy learning is likely to result in the children being viewed as linguistically, cognitively or culturally 'deficient'. Elsewhere, she calls this 'the deficit myth' (Gregory and Williams, 2000, p. 1).

Eve Gregory's view is that the national curriculum fails to acknowledge the worth of different literacy practices and the learning styles of different cultural groups. She argues that to be effective in promoting literacy in culturally diverse communities, schools have to question whether they simply want to 'transmit' the cultural norms represented by the school system (Reader 2, p. 265). She offers a positive alternative to the 'transmissionist' model (Reader 2, p. 265). She suggests that schools might choose to become knowledgeable about the strengths of their communities, using that knowledge to build bridges into school literacy practices. Schools might take their knowledge of community literacy practices as their starting point for classroom practice, for example making use of the literacy materials in the different languages that are already available to children.

'Recognizing difference', as suggested by Gregory, can lead to the transformation of school practice, as emphasis moves towards the learner and what they bring with them. In this way, diversity is seen not as a problem but as enrichment, as we saw at Bangabandhu School in Unit 5. Eve Gregory's 'bridge' links cultures and practices that are different but of equal worth. It is a perspective that emphasizes not just awareness and observation of difference, but respect for those differences, once observed. It involves partnership, where each partner is of equal worth.

3 Sure Start – a better way of working?

Making links

A major government initiative aimed at building bridges between education, families and communities is 'Sure Start'. This initiative was launched in July 1998 and aimed to bring together early education, childcare, health and family support services. As you may recall from Unit 3, Sure Start drew on American intervention programmes such as Headstart. It was part of the Government's plan to tackle childhood poverty and social exclusion, and communities to be served by Sure Start were identified using indices of deprivation. Sure Start focuses on parents as 'first educators' and as recipients of information, support and guidance, in order to help them to make the most of the developmental, learning and social potential of their child and to improve their own parenting skills. It emphasizes prevention of problems, as well as early action and intervention.

Sure Start might be seen as a top-down model, with other people, largely professionals, deciding what actions are in the best interests of those people who receive services. Catherine Ashton, Minister for Sure Start, acknowledged this focus when she described Sure Start's initial way of working:

> The first wave was very much about a new way of allowing people to work together and there are great examples – sometimes led by the health service, sometimes the education authority, always involving local people, always making sure parents got involved.

> *(Ashton quoted in Ramrayka, 2003)*

Such a focus might be seen as professionals finding better ways to work together, rather than a more radical effort to change power relationships and values. Sheila Wolfendale, for example, felt that Sure Start was potentially problematic and questioned the scheme in its early stages. She asked how far parents would be real partners in the Sure Start programmes:

> ... it remains to be seen as to whether this governmental flagship enterprise will epitomise a real partnership with parents by consulting with and including them from the earliest planning stages, through service delivery to evaluation ...

> *(Wolfendale, 2000, p. 8)*

Sheila Wolfendale herself had earlier (1985) attempted to define what 'real' partnership with parents might mean. She suggested the following criteria:

parents are active and central in decision-making and its implementation;

parents are perceived as having equal strengths and equivalent expertise;

parents are able to contribute to, as well as receive, services;

parents share responsibility, thus they and professionals are mutually accountable.

(Wolfendale, 1985, p. 14)

Evaluating Sure Start

Such partnership would involve shifts in power structures and challenges to concepts of professionalism. We have looked in Unit 3 at the 'rescue' model of provision. Some commentators have raised concerns that the Sure Start initiative too is a 'deficit–rescuing' model, which sees users of services as recipients rather than participants in decision-making. There have been concerns that Sure Start projects might stifle and replace more home-grown initiatives that had developed in response to the needs of users.

The national evaluation of Sure Start has acknowledged and investigated these concerns, with consideration in particular of how far Sure Start has 're-shaped or added value to existing service provision' and at parental involvement in the management of the new projects (Tunstill *et al.*, 2002). The report shows the diversity in structure and organization of Sure Start projects. Projects operate in different ways in different areas and with differing levels of parental involvement. While the level of parental involvement in Sure Start was found to be 'generally high', 41 per cent of the projects surveyed scored 'low' in this area (Tunstill *et al.*, 2002, pp. 2–3). Management boards included representation from statutory agencies, the voluntary sector, members of the local community and parents, but only one tenth of the programmes in the evaluation had a parent-user of the service as chair of the management board (Tunstill *et al.*, 2002, p. 2). However, the report concluded that 'There is strong evidence that good progress is being made towards developing the kinds of services parents want and need and that parents have a strong voice in shaping' (Tunstill *et al.*, 2002, p. 5).

In the next section, we shall look at how one Sure Start project in Corby, Northamptonshire, has built on existing good practice and has enabled users of services to have a major role in determining what is provided.

4 Parents shaping services

The Pen Green Centre

Until the establishment of the first blast furnace in 1910, Corby, in Northamptonshire, had been a picturesque village. After that, the development of the iron and steelworks led to rapid expansion, with a workforce drawn largely from Glasgow, Scotland. Within a few years 'Corby was transformed from a rural agricultural community into a frontier steel town' (Whalley, 1994, p. 6) and became a 'mecca for employment' in the 1970s. But this prosperity did not last: in 1980 the British Steel Corporation closed the iron and steel works. Since then, Corby has wrestled with rising levels of unemployment and the disadvantage and blight that accompanies it.

Corby and its surrounding area

The 1981 census showed that the Pen Green area of Corby was one of the most deprived areas of Northamptonshire, with poor nutrition, inadequate housing, high unemployment and high infant mortality rates. The Pen Green Centre was a response to that deprivation. It was founded in 1982 as a community-based centre for children aged under five and their families, jointly financed by the LEA, local social services and the area health authority. Margy Whalley recalls that, in the early days of the centre, there was resentment from local people who felt that there had been no consultation between officers of the County Council setting up the new services and 'the people who were supposed to use them' (Whalley, 1994, p. 9). But, from the beginning, as Margy Whalley has commented, 'we did not want to be part of a service where all the power and control was retained by the workers' (Whalley, 1994, p. 14). Consequently, the emphasis at the centre has been on parents taking a leading role in decision-making processes, through representation on management, partnership and interview panels, and participation in user groups.

Since 1982, the centre has gone through a number of transformations and has been recognized nationally as a model of good practice. It continues to work within a very mixed community, with many of its users being from potentially marginalized groups, such as teenage parents, asylum seekers, people who are long-term unemployed and people whose education, for a range of reasons, has been interrupted. In the next activity, we will watch the video about Pen Green and look at how the centre has been able to respond to and include its diverse users. We will see how the centre has offered them opportunities for change and self-development that, in turn, benefit their families and the wider community in Corby.

Pen Green was already a flourishing Early Excellence Centre when it was designated as one of the first Sure Start projects in 1998. Here, certainly, Sure Start was building on well established local networks and systems. By 2002, Pen Green served over 1,000 families on seven housing estates, and employed 38 full- and part-time workers. Margy Whalley, head of research at the centre, has pointed out that cooperation between agencies, workers and parents is not new. What was new about Pen Green, however, was the emphasis placed on relationships between those parents and workers. The development of Sure Start at Pen Green was based on consultation with local Corby families, Pen Green workers and other agencies in the local community about what services and resources were needed. As Katey Mairs, Deputy Head of the Centre, told us:

> I think the only things that have done a belly-flop at Penn Green have been the things that staff have decided would be a good idea, without actually talking to parents about how they felt about it ...
>
> *(Video Band B)*

A fundamental principle in Pen Green's work has been respect for the contribution that others might make.

Activity 9.3 Respect for others

Watch Video Band B, *Learning Together*, Part 1. This focuses on the work of the Pen Green Centre. As you watch, make notes on examples of where you see 'respect for others'. These may involve adults as well as children. How is that respect reflected in what is on offer at Pen Green?

Jimmy Kane, a former council leader who worked to build and support Pen Green over the years, identifies 'treating people as equals' and not 'talking down to them' as central to the centre's work. At the heart of the centre's work is awareness of, and responsiveness to, what the children and adults who receive the services actually want. Donna, who works at Pen Green, describes how the work of the centre is driven by its users, and initiatives have sprung from the needs of participating parents. New activities were shaped by the responses of users, as Donna comments:'We went with what they told us.'

Like a number of workers at the centre, Donna herself had initially used the centre as a parent and had made the transition to being a provider rather than receiver of its services.

Respect for individual experience lies at the heart of the centre's work. The baby massage class starts with parents asking their baby's permission before the massage can begin. For children in the nursery, such as Ben, their own activities and preferences are used as the basis of their individual programmes. For adults, there are transactional analysis classes where the subject matter is their own family interactions, as well as classes responding to individual interests, for example the desire to communicate with a deaf family member. The group discussion of the home video recording shows that a child's home experience is valued. Users and providers of services learn alongside each other, with shared experience being more important than differences in previous experiences. The physical layout of the rooms reflects the lack of hierarchy between service providers and users. Services have been set up to recognize the realities of life in Corby, with free exercise classes for those who would not be able to afford to pay, the scheduling of some groups to fit in with the shift patterns for those parents in work, and the establishment of programmes in houses on local estates for those with no transport to get to the Pen Green Centre itself. Laura, like

Donna initially a parent user of services who now works for the centre, explained how she was part of the consultation that led up to the establishment of Sure Start, talking to parents and representing them on management group.

. . . .

Learning together at Pen Green.

Long-term views

The respect for what others can contribute arises in part from long-term commitment to the centre. Many of the people we see on the video have had connections with the centre over a period many years. Bobbi describes how she was 'known' to the workers, having brought her children to Pen Green for many years. Sam talks about how she wants to 'give something back', having been given so much by the centre at an earlier point in her life. As we have already seen with Donna and Laura, people often become involved in one capacity and then move into another role.

The work of the centre, and its users, continues to change. The mothers from Croatia, for example, feel comfortable there. Users of services look forward to using the centre in different ways in the future by taking classes or becoming a paid worker.

Through national and local political changes Pen Green's workers and parents have collaborated to establish principles and set priorities. They have developed what one parent on the video describes as a 'culture'. As Margy Whalley has said, 'we learnt that if we wanted real participation then we needed to share decision making from the word go' (1994, p. 148).

 ## Activity 9.4   A genuine partnership?

Look back at page 18 and remind yourself of Sheila Wolfendale's definition of 'partnership' with parents. Then think about the following questions:

- How far does Pen Green meet the criteria Sheila Wolfendale sets?
- How is being a partner different from being a service user?

Pen Green appears to meet all the criteria set by Sheila Wolfendale. Parents are active and central to the centre's work. They contribute equal strengths and share responsibility. They play an active part in steering the direction of the centre and are not simply passive recipients of services.

Pen Green has changed and evolved over a number of years. But the philosophy and ethos has stayed the same, with respect for individuals, whether they are givers or receivers of services, or indeed both, at its centre. The professionals at Pen Green – they are called 'paid workers' – have to be prepared to give up some control of their work and to share decisions and tasks with users of the centre. They have to accept that, as paid workers, they are not necessarily the best-equipped people to carry out some tasks. The structure at Pen Green is described as one where decisions are arrived at through negotiation. Some parents (and workers!) might prefer more rapid decision making or, in some instances, a more authoritarian stance. Attitudes to smoking and drug use have been areas where there has had to be negotiation between different interest groups. Individual needs have to be weighed up in the light of the centre as a whole.

In the same way that the relationships between paid workers and parents are negotiated at Pen Green, so are the relationships between paid workers themselves, and especially those from different professional areas. Margy Whalley has pointed to the overlapping professional identities, and the different priorities that exist within different services, as factors which have held up the development of integrated services for under-fives at Pen Green. Such boundary disputes have been a challenge to the development of joined-up services not only at personal but also at local and national levels.

At Pen Green we have seen changes in the power relationships not only between paid workers and service users, but between workers from different backgrounds, for example social service workers and health professionals. Margy Whalley has commented that sometimes different departments were not used to talking to each other and often didn't appear to 'speak the same language' (1994).

Activity 9.5   Pushing back professional boundaries

Imagine that you are a 'paid worker' at Pen Green (for example a signing teacher, massage instructor or nursery teacher) working with paid workers from other professional disciplines. How might working in a multi-disciplinary team change the way you work? You may have experience in your own professional working life that will help you to reflect on this. What are the positive and negative aspects associated with this way of working? On balance, what aspects of your professional experience do you think would be enhanced?

This activity will help you with the ECA, where you are asked to explore a perspective that is not your own.

You might have noted points such as these:

- Your work might become more time consuming because it takes time to get people together.
- You might become aware of differences in perceived status between different groups and roles.
- You might find different people have different expectations of what you do and what your role entails.
- You might encounter some resentment of new ideas.
- You might develop greater awareness of what others do.
- You might acquire new knowledge as a result of crossing professional boundaries.

In the national evaluation of Sure Start, the creation of new networks and relationships, what we might call joined-up thinking, was singled out as presenting particular challenges. The evaluation recognized the following points:

- It is challenging and time consuming to join up and work in partnershipwith other agencies and providers.
- Working in multi-disciplinary teams is also a challenging task and new to many professionals.
- Sure Start programmes operate in extremely complex areas where many other initiatives operate and this exacerbates

the issues around collaborative working for most programmes.

(Tunstill et al., 2002, p. 6)

As we pointed out at the start of this section, Pen Green started off as a top-down initiative. But, as we have seen, twenty years on there is a sense at Pen Green of the services being bottom up or user-driven, and it is widely acknowledged that these services are responsive to the local community. Robert, who you saw in the video leading the transactional analysis group, gave us an example of that responsiveness:

> My educational background's in special needs and visual impairment. And I was asked to look at a little girl in nursery who wasn't speaking, and I watched her for a few minutes and thought, 'yes – she's either deaf or has a language difficulty' ... So we got a local teacher of the hearing impaired in and within a few minutes she was diagnosed as severely deaf and within a week I think our Wider Opportunities crew had recruited a teacher of sign language, so I went along ... [I] have done a deaf awareness course and got my certificate to show now that I have some extra skills in communicating with a deaf child. And I think that's perhaps the strength of our adult education course here. It identifies where there might be some interest and a need and responds very quickly – we'll find a tutor, and now there is a British Sign Language course running here ...

Such user-driven ways of working have taken many years to evolve; they depend on a well-established culture, which is known and respected and which, in the end, overrides the differences between individuals. In the next section of the unit, we look at specific initiatives that are aiming to create structures that are equally responsive to communities and individuals. We might describe these initiatives as top down, though they are viewed by those who are initiating them as long-term projects that will engage with the service users and in time be owned by them.

5 Joining up services

The growing understanding that cooperative working can improve professional effectiveness has now become embodied in government policies in both England and Scotland. In England, the 2003 Green Paper *Every Child Matters*, which made proposals about how services should be brought together, called for 'radical reform' to break down

Collecting data at Pen Green.

'organisational boundaries' (DfES, 2003, p. 9). The Green Paper commented:

> We want to value the specific skills that people from different professional backgrounds bring, and we also want to break down the professional barriers that inhibit joint working.
>
> *(DfES, 2003, p. 10)*

Many of the proposals for changes in practice in England were already in place in Scotland and we will turn next to look at an example of a joined-up initiative in Scotland.

The full service school model in North Lanarkshire

In 1985, at about the time that Pen Green was being established, the Strathclyde region of Scotland made a major investment in education for children aged under five through the radical reorganization of all its under-five services. The flagship of the new policy was the establishment of community nurseries, which were intended to cater for the entire under-five age group in the areas they served and to act as a social and educational resource for children, parents, families and communities. The underlying principle of the reorganization was that care and education would be combined: there would be 'one door' for parents, voluntary and community groups and health authorities.

By 1996, when local government reorganization created North Lanarkshire out of parts of what had been Strathclyde, 'excellent practice was widespread' in under-five education (Boyd and O'Neill, 1999, p. 53). In addition, the council took seriously the principle of pupil involvement in decision making, and supported parent forums and curriculum materials targeted at parents. Brian Boyd, an academic at the University of Strathclyde, and Michael O'Neill, Director of Education in North Lanarkshire, describe how the newly created North Lanarkshire council, which was committed to tackling pupil underachievement, drew on these existing principles, while moving forward with the creation of new structures.

Boyd and O'Neill describe the awareness that existed within the LEA that initiatives for raising achievement needed go beyond the classroom. That idea, in the USA, had given rise to the 'full service school', where parents and pupils have access to a full range of non-educational as well as educational services. The concept of a full service school was central to the provision that they wished to put in place locally. Boyd and O'Neill use Corrigan's description of the full service school as 'a "seamless" institution, a community school with a joint governance structure that allows maximum responsiveness to families and communities and promotes accessibility and continuity for those most in need of the services' (Corrigan, 1997, quoted in Boyd and O'Neill, 1999, p. 54).

The full service school springs from a concept of education that is:

- child centred,
- family-focused,
- community-based,
- culturally sensitive.

(Corrigan, 1997, quoted in Boyd and O'Neill, 1999, p. 54)

Boyd and O'Neill were also aware of the work of Joy Dryfoos, who has described the development of the full service school in the USA, where school buildings were used as places to integrate education, medical, social and/or human services targeted at growing numbers of disadvantaged young people and their families (Dryfoos, 1995, p. 147). Full service schools have developed in the USA as neighbourhood schools have found it increasingly difficult to educate pupils and at the same time deal with the social problems their pupils bring with them. She describes how 'everywhere ... the school house doors have opened' (Dryfoos, 1995, p. 153), with at least forty different types of personnel now working in schools, including nurses, clergy and community police. In the USA, the idea of the full service school has acted as a catalyst for educational initiatives, as it simultaneously addresses the need for 'individual support, comprehensive services, parent involvement and community improvement' (Dryfoos, 1995, p. 167). The full service school has been a way to remove barriers that have an impact on education, such as those arising from poor housing, health or social problems.

In North Lanarkshire, a range of initiatives was developed to target individual and community need in a way similar to the initiatives described by Joy Dryfoos. Targeted resources accompanied these initiatives and were allocated through indices of deprivation. The initiatives focused on early intervention, raising self-esteem through Outward Bound and theatre-based projects, and the celebration of success through artistic, sporting and musical events.

As the North Lanarkshire project developed, it was underpinned by the following principles, many of which you will recognize as principles central to inclusive education and many of which we have already seen in action at Pen Green:

- all individuals are of equal worth and have equal rights to have their needs met and their potential developed;
- diversity in the background, belief systems, and lifestyles of learners should be respected and celebrated;
- the development of self-esteem and a positive sense of community is critical in raising achievement;
- education is a lifelong process;
- education should be concerned with the development of the whole person and with preparation for citizenship and other adult roles;
- people learn best when they are able to understand and guide their own learning;
- raising achievement should be seen as a fundamental aim of education;
- education can make a crucial difference to achievement.

(Boyd and O'Neill, 1999, p. 56)

The working group that developed policy and practice in North Lanarkshire was diverse, with representatives from all phases of schooling, the psychological services, community education, learning support, personnel from home–school links, trade unions and local business. Boyd and O'Neill describe the project as 'a journey'. They cite the council's policy:

> It should be stressed that the departmental strategy to raise achievement represents a long-term commitment to which all members of the education service, parents, and the wider community are asked to subscribe.

(Boyd and O'Neill, 1999, p. 57)

In this enterprise, working together is the key to creating a new kind of relationship out of the existing elements of their community. These existing elements, Boyd and O'Neil argue, are transformed by being brought together in a new way.

But does bringing professionals together inevitably lead to individual and community empowerment of a sort we saw at Pen Green? Is professional collaboration the way to energize and revitalize potentially marginalized groups? The next sections in this unit examine these questions through a study of New Community Schools in Scotland.

The New Community Schools initiative

North Lanarkshire's initiative on working together had been underway for about eighteen months when, in November 1998, the Scottish Executive launched its own New Community Schools (NCS) initiative. This launched 62 pilot projects, with 2 community schools in each of Scotland's 32 local councils, with the exception of Orkney and Shetland.

The underpinning philosophy of the initiative is described on the NCS website. The community schools reflect a 'multi-disciplinary, cross-cutting' approach and 'put at the centre the interests of the individual child':

> They embody the fundamental principle that the potential of all children can be realised only by addressing their needs in the round. In New Community Schools, teachers, social workers, community education workers, health professionals and others work together in a single team to meet the needs of the individual child.
>
> *(Scottish Executive, 2002)*

The prospectus published in 1998 by the Scottish Office Education and Industry Department set out the following as 'essential characteristics' of projects funded under the scheme:

- a focus on the needs of all pupils;
- engagement with families;
- engagement with the wider community;
- integrated provision of school education, informal as well as formal education, social work, and health education and promotion services;
- integrated management;
- arrangements for the delivery of these services according to a set of integrated objectives and measurable outcomes;
- commitment and leadership;
- multi-disciplinary training and staff development.

You might find it useful to keep this list to hand as you complete the next activity, in which we watch the next part of Video Band B. This focuses on Bannockburn High School, a New Community School near Stirling.

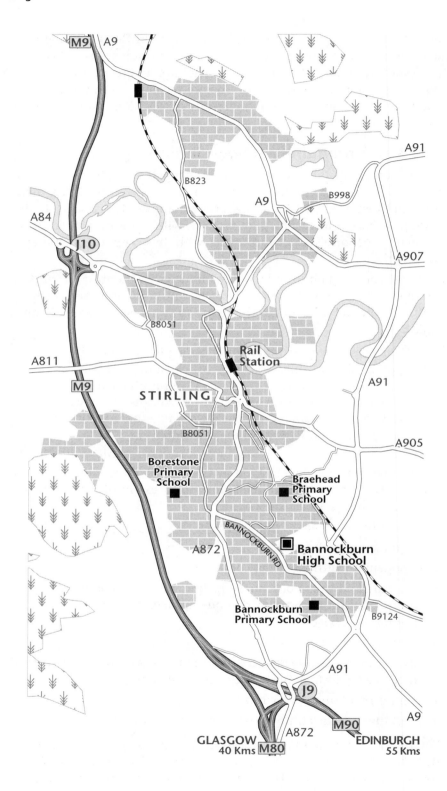

Location of Bannockburn.

◯ Activity 9.6   Participation

Now watch Video Band B, *Learning Together*, Part 2.

As you watch, make notes on what 'participation' means at Bannockburn High School. Then think about what the similarities and differences are between practice at Bannockburn and practice that we saw at Pen Green in Section 4.

If we look first at similarities, respect for individuals and groups of people is a key feature underpinning practice at Bannockburn High School, as it was at Pen Green. At Bannockburn respect is literally central to the school's 'CARES' philosophy:

Confidence

Achievement

Respect

Expectations

Standards

Jim McAlpine, Bannockburn's headteacher, says respect is 'ingrained in our philosophy'. At both Pen Green and Bannockburn High School this basic philosophy pre-dates any current structures and is the springboard for what actually goes on in the school. In both settings there are leaders who share commitment to what we might call 'big ideas' – the common good and the welfare of others. At Pen Green, Jimmy Kane calls this 'making good citizens' and believes that what the centre does is integral to the future development of Corby.

This sense of respect for others, at both Pen Green and Bannockburn, leads to an openness about what different people can contribute to the school and to each other. Education is not all one way: 'givers' can learn from 'receivers'. Jim McAlpine identifies respect as what the school has learned from its experience of pupils with physical disabilities. We hear about how the school responded with great sensitivity to the death of a pupil, Gary. His mother comments: 'He must have given a lot back to the school if they want to do a prize.' She tells us about how the school has respected her knowledge of her children's needs.

We see at Bannockburn members of the school's local community participating in mentoring pupils. One mentor had previously been a pupil at the school and was returning in a different capacity. The school deliberately draws on local resources, inviting local people to help with clubs.

Young people are encouraged to contribute their views about the running of the school. We see the school council in action. The pupils clearly set a high value on the council and compete to be elected. Older pupils support younger ones in lessons, adding another dimension to their learning which does not involve a teacher, and extending their own understanding of the learning process while doing so. The sixth former who is helping in the music lesson movingly describes his own reaction when a pupil he is helping suddenly understands: 'The looks on their faces when they're dein' it ... It's hard to explain ... a kind of joy.'

A striking feature of the Bannockburn video, and a significant difference from what we saw in Corby, is the way professionals gather at regular meetings. They describe the projects underway in their areas and the structures that, they hope, will draw in more parents and pupils to what is on offer. 'Participation' here might be defined in professional terms, with 'providers' organizing events for 'users'. 'Users' of services are not present at these meetings and we

Bannockburn High School student council at work.

only hear about them, not from them. This is a marked contrast to Pen Green. However, Jim McAlpine looks forward to the day when users of services will set their own agenda rather than simply responding to what others provide for them, when 'Families and children will wish to start organizing their own activities'.

There are signs from the video that this might be happening, initially in the primary schools that are part of the Bannockburn cluster of schools. Jim McAlpine identifies these primary activities and we hear Chris describe them on the video. She describes how the children's committee, drawn from a range of local primary schools, is setting up a children's conference, deciding on its own venue and activities. In addition, parents and local volunteers are joining in projects in surrounding villages.

At Bannockburn High School itself, the school council is well established and takes its role seriously, though there is a sense on the video that it still operates within very clearly prescribed parameters. As one pupil comments, 'Mr McAlpine's letting pupils take over.' We see the council discussing toilets and the school's domestic arrangements, not looking at how teaching is organized or how pupils learn best. This is despite the clear evidence from one of the pupils, Scott, of the powerful insights that young learners can have into their own learning and into the classroom situations where, in his view, he has been effectively included.

We need to bear in mind, however, that the video is extremely short and the NCS initiative is a recent one, in comparison to the long-established practices at Pen Green. In both settings, time, trust and commitment are seen as central to the development of good practices and to the involvement of the wider community. Jim

McAlpine and Jimmy Kane both see what they are doing as part of a long-term effort to improve the local community. There are no 'quick ways' to participation.

A marked feature for us in the Pen Green video is the sense we have of personal and community change, brought about by involvement with the centre. We saw, for example, numerous transitions from parent user of the centre to paid worker. A number of people spoke about the personal change they experienced through their contact with Pen Green.

In Bannockburn, through constraints of time, we were not able to talk to any 'users' of services, for example, people who took part in the projects described by the professionals at their meeting. So we have few examples of this sort of personal empowerment, though we catch glimpses of it in school in our interview with Scott and with the sixth former supporting the music lesson.

 ## Activity 9.7   Asking questions

Imagine that you are the parent of a pupil at Bannockburn High School. There is going to be a meeting that parents can attend to find out more about the NCS initiative. It is likely that as a parent you may have heard the mention of New Community Schools in the local media, but you are likely to be unaware of the details of this initiative. What are the things that you would want to know about it as a parent? Jot down the questions that you would like to ask at the meeting. Try to think of at least four questions.

This activity will be useful preparation for the examinable component of this course, in helping you to draft questions that will elicit information about areas with which you have no previous familiarity.

 It may be that as a parent you feel you have little understanding of what the new ways of working are and you would first want to ask quite basic questions. What are the main changes that are going to happen at the school because of the initiative? How will this affect my child? What new things are going to be available to my child because of the initiative? Is everyone at the school entitled to these things?

You may also want to ask about how the teachers' ways of working have changed as a result of the initiative. You may want to know how the initiative is being evaluated, for example in terms of rates of exclusion or improved health. You may want to know how you, as a parent, can influence what may seem to you a 'professionally driven' venture. How will the community take ownership of the project? Will the project continue when direct funding ceases?

Jim McAlpine sees the NCS initiative as a project with a long-term future, during which practice within the school will be transformed. At this point, it is not possible to say how far the aims of the project will eventually be 'owned' by those who are receiving services. Early evaluation of the NCS initiative reports that community engagement is the least developed feature of the NCS initiative in Scotland.

The issue is encapsulated by the interchange we see between Janice (whose clothing logo may or may not reflect her own view of her academic status) and her mentor. Janice has been 'given' her well-meaning mentor and she accepts her with resignation and good grace. But will the relationship that the mentor hopes to build up enable Janice to take an active part in her own education and in decisions about the future? Will Janice move from being passive to active in her own education and will her capacity to participate increase? We don't know. You might like to watch that section of the video again – what do you think? Is Janice being given something she sees as necessary to her life?

● ● ● ● ● ● ● ● ● ● ● ● ● ● ● ● ● ● ●

The issues raised in this video about the relationship between users and providers of services are ones that have been discussed by commentators in relation to the NCS initiative as a whole. Jon Nixon, Julie Allan and Gregory Mannion, for example, have pointed out that 'there are serious difficulties in attempting to collapse a potentially radical community action agenda into a mildly progressive agenda emphasizing coordinated service provision and professional collaboration' (Nixon, Allan and Mannion, 2001, p. 330). They continue:

> Joined-up policy, to adopt the jargon, may be desirable, but it does not itself guarantee the devolution of power from policy-makers and professional practitioners to community leaders and parents.
>
> *(Nixon, Allan and Mannion, 2001, p. 330)*

In the 30 local authorities their study looked at, 'community participation' meant very different things and ranged from limited consultation with parents by professionals, to the establishment of community-led groups that had a direct input into the development of NCS in their area. As one of their interviewees put it:

> If you want to bring about social change that means anything, you actually have to involve the folk that you expect the social change to come from.
>
> *(Nixon, Allan and Mannion, 2001, p. 339)*

Professionals working together at Bannockburn High School.

One of the barriers to involvement of people who used the services which the researchers identified was the deficit-based view of the local area and of the capacity of its inhabitants which was held by some professionals and voluntary workers.

One of the ways that participation of pupils could be developed is through the Personal Learning Plans (PLP) that are a feature of the NCS initiative, though not part of what we filmed at Bannockburn. Jon Nixon and his colleagues collected considerable data about PLPs and saw them as a major agent for developing pupil participation in education and in their community. They interviewed an LEA officer, who described what the PLP is about:

> It's not the teacher's document, it's the child's document
> – where they specify targets for themselves within school
> but also outwith school. So, if they're involved in an out
> of school club or sports activity, they can invite comment
> from coaches, wherever they're working, or other adult
> helpers to tell them how well they're doing. But the
> children set the targets for the next week, not just in
> terms of educational attainment, but they set themselves
> targets for outwith school activity, perhaps home activity,
> perhaps health and fitness ...
>
> *(Nixon, Allan and Mannion, 2001, p. 341)*

The young people themselves recognized that the PLPs belonged to them:

> It's like homework because you take it home and you do it
> at home and you've got to think about it. And it's not like
> homework because it feels more personal because when

you're doing your homework it's like you've all got the same problem, maybe with a sentence or something like that. But here it's your own comments and your own suggestions.

(Nixon, Allan and Mannion, p. 342)

Within the NCS initiative, then, there is the potential, at a number of points, for the realization of the more radical agenda that we saw in action at the Pen Green Centre in Corby, where learners themselves take responsibility for their own learning and where there are shifts in where power resides. The NCS initiative is still in its early stages and as the project beds down we will be in a position to evaluate how far this develops from being a top-down to a bottom-up initiative.

Activity 9.8   Crystal ball

What might be happening at Bannockburn High School in ten years time? Jot down some of the changes you might expect to see if the community comes to own this initiative.

Blueprint for the future?

The idea of the school as a hub for multi-agency working is currently developing rapidly in England. The Green Paper, *Every Child Matters*, for example, envisages a full service school in every local authority by 2006 (DfES, 2003).

Robin Bishop, an architect and director of Effective Learning Environments, a consultancy specializing in innovative educational and related design, has written about how school buildings can nurture participation by opening up 'opportunities for multi-agency working and community enrichment' (Bishop, 2001, p. 58). One of his case studies is Millennium Primary School in Greenwich, which combines both a school and a health centre. You have already looked at the ground-floor plans for Millennium Primary School in Unit 3. The primary school is for 420 pupils aged 4–11 years old, and offers ' "designated special provision" for a group of children with autistic spectrum disorder' (Bishop, 2001, p. 60). Robin Bishop describes the project:

> Education and health care are on one site, offering a range of related services for early years, special educational needs, child care, family support, lifelong learning and the community ... The school has its own early years centre ... and a creche for the use of parents attending the health centre or other activities in the school ... There is disabled access to all parts of the two-storey complex, and

rooms for SEN support and hygiene. Physiotherapy and other services are available in the health centre ...

(Bishop, 2001, p. 60)

In its physical construction, Millennium Primary School has been designed as a full service school and as the focal point of the developing community. The facility includes a one-stop shop for advice and information and also offers adult education and training opportunities. Out of school hours the school facilities (for example the hall, studio, changing rooms, all-weather pitch and the library) are open for community use. In addition to primary care, the GPs based in the health centre provide some secondary facilities more usually found in hospitals. The health centre also promotes healthy living and preventative approaches to medicine.

 ## Activity 9.9   Pause for thought

Think about the ways in which the blueprint for Millennium Primary School reminds you of Pen Green. In what ways does it seem different? If you were asked to estimate how successful the Millennium initiative had been, what questions would you like to ask?

The building of Millennium Primary School was supported by a range of agencies, including the Department for the Environment, Transport and Regions, and Greenwich Council, which closed an existing school and transferred pupils to the new building. Like Pen Green, it houses a number of services so that parents can access health and social workers, for example, in one location. Pen Green, in its various forms, has been developing since 1982, while Millennium Primary School is a very recent project and as yet there has not been time for this top-down initiative to be claimed and owned by local people.

In evaluating the Millennium Primary School project, we might want to know how local people have been consulted and how they now feel about the services that are available. Do any parents of children with additional needs see the provision on offer at the centre as the medicalization of their children's early years experiences? Have parents, for example, made an opportunity to shape how services are provided? How have parents and service users made this 'blueprint' their own, when it was developed by professionals from outside their communities? Do they feel they need the services that are provided? What services do they feel they need? Were children consulted about how they learn best?

We discussed in Unit 7 how small-scale research projects have succeeded in drawing out from children insights into how and in what settings they feel comfortable and learn best. One such research project was that carried out by Vanessa Penrose, Gary Thomas and Clara Greed (2001). While the results of their study are very interesting and give new and informative insights into how children view their learning, the methods used by the research team are in themselves innovative and interesting. If we are to move towards learning structures where learners 'recognize themselves', then innovative research methods of this kind are important, since they give insights into the perspectives and reactions of people whose views are rarely recorded.

The researchers conducted interviews with thirteen children and young people of various ages. They were a diverse group: three had hearing impairments; three had visual impairments; two had been identified by their school as having behavioural difficulties; one had a physical impairment; and four were not disabled. They were asked questions and were also asked to respond to photographs and drawings, taped sounds and samples of smells that may be associated with aspects of school. The children were also asked to engage in various kinds of visual and non-visual imaging exercises. A major part of the project involved gathering the stimuli – photographs, sounds and smells – that would trigger responses.

Methodology was extremely important since, in the words of the researchers:

> One of the main objectives of this project was to investigate the most effective way in which children and young people with special needs could be encouraged to express honest and understandable opinions about their school.
>
> *(Penrose, Thomas and Greed, 2001, p. 89)*

Without exception, the children noted the aesthetic features of their environments, for example colour, light and windows, cluttered classrooms, size of outside spaces, and differences between sun and shade outside. These aspects elicited more significant reactions than more practical and functional aspects of the environment, such as carpets or low ceilings. The researchers also found that there were fewer differences between the sub-groups of children than they had expected. They recommend that ethnographic research, where children are 'shadowed' round schools and their interactions and reactions are noted, might give useful insights into how children view their learning environments. As John Davis and Nick Watson pointed out:

> ... disabled children, whatever their impairment, can be competent participants in every day decision making processes when they are provided with opportunities to

interact with other children on an equitable basis, their participation is properly planned and not reliant on short term adult assessments of competency, and when they are able to work with reflexive adults. By this, we mean adults who understand that disabled children, like other children and adults, are flexible social beings whose behavioural patterns, communication abilities, level of involvement and level of interest will vary over the duration of an activity.

(Davis and Watson, 2000, p. 213)

It may be that research of this kind will give a lead to the creation of settings where the full diversity of children and young people, including marginalized groups, not only participate more fully but also 'recognize themselves'.

6 Shifts in power

We saw at Pen Green that users can make a major impact on the way services develop. At Bannockburn, we saw pupils taking part in decision making about the way their school was run. In this next section, we look further at how young peoples' experiences, in inclusive settings, can be become part of planning for the future.

Pupils bringing about change

Chris Searle, formerly head teacher of Earl Marshal school in Sheffield, has written about how his school community itself began to forge new networks to prevent marginalization and exclusion. Earl Marshal School served the families of ex-steelworkers, as well as 'the arrivant peoples of Pakistan, Yemen, the Caribbean and Somalia' (Searle, 2001, p. 53). The school involved governors and community organizations in new networks, via the Sheffield Black Community Forum, which worked vigorously to oppose permanent exclusion of pupils. In addition, pupils organized themselves into new networks. Chris Searle describes how serious tension had developed between boys from the Pakistani and Somali communities, with group fights taking place during dinner hours and after school. Teachers' efforts had proved ineffectual, until young Yemenis came forward and took the initiative:

The Yemeni school students called some influential members from the Pakistani and Somali boys' groups together for a crowded meeting, sitting around the large table in my office. I left them to it. After over two hours of passionate discussions (they could be heard well beyond the office walls) the students emerged, clasping each other's hands and claiming that they had resolved the problems between them. The young Yemenis ... had become the peacemakers in a Yorkshire city on another continent ... And they had done it themselves. Nobody was excluded, and although there was a residual tension between many of the boys of both communities, the hostility and suspicion gradually dissipated.

(Searle, 2001, p. 72)

The community itself responded to problems the school experienced with truanting pupils. Chris Searle tells the story of how truanting pupils tended to congregate in a neighbouring Yemeni café, where the adult customers were largely illiterate Yemeni ex-steelworkers who had been made redundant during the collapse of the steel industry in the early 1980s. A Pakistani teacher of Urdu offered to spend several hours a week in the café, teaching its customers basic English. Chris Searle writes:

> The owner was enthusiastic, the classes were well attended, and the student users ... kept well away, some of them even returning to school and pursuing their studies with greater commitment ... By such strategies too, we found support in the place we really needed and wanted it – in the streets and estates around the school.

(Searle, 2001, p. 153)

As had happened at Corby, a powerful catalyst of change was the fact that the solutions to community problems were found within the resources of the community itself.

Real partnership?

Earlier in this unit we have questioned, in relation to the Sure Start initiative, whether parents and children are genuinely viewed as equals by professionals and how far they are seen simply as the recipients of services. We have argued that for services to be truly inclusive users of those services need to have control and input into what is on offer, and to be partners as defined by Sheila Wolfendale. But the term partnership has often been used rhetorically and has become something of a cliché. Gillian Fulcher (1989) has put forward the challenging idea that the concept of 'parents as partners', within the context of special education law, simply brings parents into the bureaucratic procedures of the state. She argues that such partnership, far from giving parents an equal part in the decision-making system, simply serves to facilitate the smooth operation of the bureaucratic procedures themselves. Parents in this context are 'co-opted' not invited to participate. It is probably for this reason that some parents simply refuse to participate in the bureaucratic processes open to them. As one parent of a disabled child put it:

If I have a problem getting my child into the mainstream school that I want, when he's 11, I wouldn't dream of going to the Tribunal. Why do that? Waste of time. I'd arrange a demo.

(Sunita, a parent, personal communication with the author)

Richard Rieser, in Chapter 16 of Reader 1, is dismissive of being expected to participate in other peoples' agendas, preferring to be part of an agenda set by disabled adults.

When we were thinking about Bannockburn High School in Section 5 of this unit, we considered the question of whether bringing together professionals actually made any difference to the experience of service users. There were no parents or users sitting round the table at the staff meeting we watched. We wondered whether 'partnership' really brought benefits to anyone other than professionals. Evaluation of the NCS initiative has shown that in some areas there has been real community engagement with new projects but in others professionals remained in control, consulting only within existing frameworks.

A Bannockburn parent, pupil and teacher meet to discuss progress.

The challenges in implementing joined-up thinking and the issues raised about joint professional working and genuine participation are not just felt at grass roots or even at service-planning level. They are found also at government level, as policies are developed. An unusual and fascinating insight into government policy processes was given by Norman Glass, a senior civil servant who was part of the cross-departmental review process that led to the Sure Start initiative.

In an article that describes how Sure Start was established, Glass shows how, for the first time, senior civil servants were brought into personal contact with some of the people and projects that would be directly affected by emerging policies. Senior officials and service users at first found it strange to work together and were mutually suspicious of hidden agendas:

> Because of the wide range of departments involved in the Review and because the Treasury had been one of its principal advocates, it was decided that the Treasury should chair the Review and provide its secretariat. This aroused some initial suspicions among other departments that the exercise would be directed towards seeking cuts in programmes and at first departments tended to be represented on the Review by finance officials but as suspicion lessened these were gradually replaced by officials from the relevant policy divisions.

> *(Glass, 1999, p. 259)*

More boundaries had to be crossed when policy development opened up to include the voluntary sector, existing projects and academics. Even the venues for meetings presented challenges to participants.

> The first seminar was held at the Treasury and there was a slightly comic atmosphere as the two worlds of children's services and Gladstonian public finance met face to face. The trepidation felt by the early years' community was probably only matched by the bewilderment of the Treasury doorkeepers faced with directing people to a seminar on services for young children. Perhaps they felt, recalling Jonathan Swift and his Modest Proposal, that the Treasury intention was to find a way of cooking the children and serving them up as a cheap and nutritious diet supplement!

> *(Glass, 1999, p. 261)*

Norman Glass tells us that the development of Sure Start was striking because of the way that it involved people outside central government and brought in many users of the services under discussion. The consultation process, which included a stakeholders' conference involving ministers and 250 delegates, helped to ensure that the developers of a radical, cross-departmental strategy interacted directly with users of services.

In recent years, there has been increasing interest in the question of how users of services, in particular children who are likely to be affected by processes of marginalization, might be enabled to contribute to policy development and to their own education and lives. Answers have been both structural, that is to do with local and national policy development, and more local, for example where schools examine ways that children can engage more directly with their own learning processes.

What further structures might be needed across the UK was a subject addressed by Rachel Hodgkin and Peter Newell in a 1996 report funded by the Gulbenkian Foundation. They concluded that children were invisible, with no obvious place in central government policies. The introduction to the report comments on 'how modest is the extent of formal inter-ministerial and inter-departmental co-ordination for children within current structures' (Hodgkin and Newell, 1996, p. 5). Children had no political priority:

> There is no annual report on the state of UK children, no systematic collection or publication of statistics, no requirement to assess and publish information on the impact of government policies on children and no analysis of overall or departmental budgets to assess the amount and proportion spent on children.
>
> *(Hodgkin and Newell, 1996, p. 13)*

A major finding of the report was that coordination between government departments themselves, and between Whitehall and government departments in Northern Ireland, Scotland and Wales was inadequate. The report found that many respondents in the study singled out many serious problems relating to poor inter-departmental coordination:

> Many conformed to the definition of what have been termed 'wicked issues' – intractably complex issues where the nature of the problem and the solution are not fully understood, and which involve more than one department and are not dealt with satisfactorily by any.
>
> *(Hodgkin and Newell, 1996, p. 14)*

Further, they found that government structures inhibited flexibility of funding, both at central and at local levels, and that there are few structures that promote children's participation in society.

Rachel Hodgkin and Peter Newell put forward a number of proposals to improve structures for children. Their key recommendations were as follows:

1   A governmental strategy for UK children which would provide the overall aims and objectives, programmes and targets for children.

2   Child impact analysis should be built into all government strategies.

3   There should be coordination of government for children, including a standing inter-ministerial group on children and coordination between central and local government.

4   Children's active participation should be promoted. The principle that children should take an active part in decision making is generally accepted and this should therefore be implemented. Serious consideration should be given to lowering the voting age to 16.

5   The creation of a senior ministerial post with a seat in Cabinet which would have responsibility for children and direct responsibility for a Cabinet Office Children's Unit.

6   In Parliament there should be a 'special focus' Select Committee on Children in the Commons, and a Select Committee on the Needs of Children and their Families in the House of Lords.

7   There should be an independent Children's Rights Commissioner, who would be tasked with influencing law, policy and practice; reviewing children's access to advocacy and complaints systems; conducting investigations; undertaking or encouraging research; and promoting awareness of rights among children and adults.

Rachel Hodgkin and Peter Newell carried out their work in 1996. Since then there has been considerable change at government policy level. We have seen in earlier units that the principle of young people's participation have been emphasized in, for example, the 2001 *Special Educational Needs Code of Practice* (DfES, 2001), where the participation of young people has been given high priority, though not a stronger legal basis. Initiatives like Sure Start and Connexions, for pupils over the age of fourteen, have brought together different areas of government.

The 2003 Green Paper, *Every Child Matters*, which is part of the government's response to the death of Victoria Climbie, is a radical move forward in joining up services for children. It addresses a number of the issues raised by Rachel Hodgkin and Peter Newell and proposes new legislation that would bring together multiple agencies in a child-centred way. Paul Boateng, Chief Secretary to the Treasury, writes in the Introduction to the Green Paper:

> We will be called upon to make common cause across professional boundaries and with reformed structures and services to create the means by which the needs, interests and welfare of children can be better protected and advanced.
>
> *(DfES, 2003, p. 4)*

Among the proposals in the Green Paper are the promotion of full service schools (of the sort we have seen at Bannockburn and in the NCS initiative) and the creation of a new Children's Commissioner 'to act as an independent champion for children, particularly those suffering disadvantage' (DfES, 2003, p. 10). This post is not necessarily conceived of in the same way as the children's rights commissioner proposed by Rachel Hodgkin and Peter Newell. The role of the national Children's Commissioner is, at the time of writing, as yet undeveloped. However, the proposal itself represents a considerable shift in government thinking.

Ianthe Maclagan was one of the first locally appointed children's rights commissioners. She was appointed to work at strategic policy level in Oxfordshire, with a brief that covered all children in Oxfordshire. The Commissioner works across agencies, including education, social services and health services. Children and young people were involved in the interviewing process for the post. As the post has developed, the views of children and young people have been central to the process of change. Their views were sought, for example, as part of a needs assessment and over 600 children and young people responded by way of questionnaires and focus groups. Some of the questions focused on whether children felt they were listened to. One participant said of teachers: 'They think they're better than us because we're younger than them' (Maclagan, 2002, p. 135). The Commissioner's vision for the future is clear: 'for Oxfordshire to become a county where children's rights are flagged up wherever you look, underpin all policy and practice, and can never be forgotten' (Maclagan, 2002, p. 137).

However, these policy initiatives have not necessarily enabled young people to become more active participants in their own learning. John Quicke, for example, has pointed out that some initiatives may have the reverse effect and may actually 'become a way of legitimising a very limited view of participation' (Quicke, 2003, p. 51). Writing about the *Special Educational Needs Code of Practice* and its emphasis on pupil participation, John Quicke notes:

> [Pupils] are also to be asked about their views on their own needs and difficulties in contributions to statutory assessments and annual review meetings. The importance of participation is acknowledged but largely confined to involvement in formal procedures. At a time when the value of such procedures is being questioned even this limited involvement may not be in the pupils' best interests. We might even be asking pupils to collude in their own negative labelling'
>
> *(Quicke, 2003, p. 51)*

Quicke's alternative is to encourage pupil participation through reflection on their own learning, a process that we have seen to some extent in the PLPs in Scotland.

He describes how pupils can be encouraged to reflect on themselves as individual learners, on themselves as part of a group, on their relationships with their teachers and on how they learn in informal settings, for instance at home. Their reflections would be prompted by questions, such as:

How do I remember things?

How do I learn from my mistakes?

How do I help others and how do others help me?

How do I let my teacher know about my views and experiences?

How do I learn at home?

How did I learn from my brothers and sisters?

Learning how to learn is an open-ended exploratory process in which the young person becomes an active participant. Underlying the process is Quicke's view of inclusion:

> Inclusive philosophy requires us to see the pupil, and the teacher for that matter, as an agent (i.e. as someone who can become independent, active and empowered) interacting with others in a social context to produce a community in which everyone is a participant and everyone is empowered.
>
> *(Quicke, 2003, p. 52)*

Older pupils offer support at Bannockburn High School.

You may be reminded at this point of Jimmy Kane's view that Pen Green was about making young people independent and active, with the ability to make changes for the better in their own lives:

> Well [education's] about preparing young people to be good citizens and to be able to stand on their own two feet and be able to do what they think is necessary. I had an illustration of this given to me, two illustrations. Some of the children from here go to different primary schools or infant schools and one of the schools they went to, they said that they were too bossy and they, you know, they were a bit bolshie for ... young people. And I thought that was terribly sad, but I was comforted because I then received [another view] direct from another headteacher,

and they said the best children that come into this school are in fact the children that come through Pen Green. They're independent. They know what they want to do. And if they're like that, then they'll certainly make their way in the world much better.

7 Conclusion

Independent, active, participating, equal – these words have occurred again and again in this unit. To enable learners to take on any, or all, of these qualities can sometimes challenge existing structures and traditional ideas of hierarchies and power. This is another vision of what inclusive education is and should be all about. We have seen that the systems that seem effective in nurturing such learners are open, participatory and flexible. But they are underpinned by clear values and philosophical frameworks where respect for others and their differences is paramount. Pen Green and Bannockburn High School have many differences, yet they have much in common. Both enjoy strong leadership based on an underpinning commitment to social improvement – the 'big idea' of the common good and the welfare of others.

In the course of their work on NCS, Nixon and his colleagues interviewed the Director of Children's Services in a Scottish LEA. He said:

> I cannot empower anybody. Nobody. Who empowered Vaclev Havel or Nelson Mandela? But I do want to create the circumstances in which people can exercise their professional or community responsibilities by seeking empowerment. I think that's very different. We structured NCS with a potential for radicalism ... I think they'll surprise themselves.
>
> *(Quoted in Nixon, Allan and Mannion, 2001, p. 347)*

At Pen Green, we have seen people being surprised by what they have achieved, often after years of failure and marginalization. At Bannockburn work is in progress, with plans to change the school both through new buildings and extended capacity. As Jim McAlpine said:

> My belief is that with working with all the agencies and all the families and members of the community in this school, in five or ten years time we will say, 'We have moved forward.'

References

Bishop, R. (2001) 'Designing for special educational needs in mainstream schools', *Support for Learning*, **16**(2), p. 56–63.

Boyd, B. and O'Neill, M. (1999) 'Raising achievement for all: North Lanarkshire's strategy for breaking the links between disadvantage and underachievement', *Support for Learning*, **14**(2), pp. 51–7.

Davis, J. and Watson, N. (2000) 'Disabled children's rights in every day life: problematising notions of competency and promoting self-empowerment', *International Journal of Children's Rights*, **8**, pp. 211–28

Department for Education and Skills (DfES) (2001) *Special Educational Needs Code of Practice*, London, DfES.

Department for Education and Skills (DfES) (2003) *Every Child Matters*, London, HMSO.

Dryfoos, J.G. (1995) 'Full service schools: revolution or fad?', *Journal of Research on Adolescence*, **5**(2), pp. 147–72.

Fulcher, G. (1989) *Disabling Policies: a comparative approach to educational policy and disability*, London, Falmer.

Glass, N. (1999) 'Sure Start: the development of an early intervention programme for young children in the UK', *Children and Society*, **13**(4), pp. 257–64.

Gregory, E. and Williams, A. (2000) *City Literacies*, London, Routledge.

Hodgkin, R. and Newell, P. (1996) *Effective Government Structures for Children: report of a Gulbenkian Foundation inquiry*, London, Calouste Gulbenkian Foundation.

Lloyd, G. and Norris, C. (1998) 'From difference to deviance: the exclusion of gypsy-traveller children from school in Scotland', *International Journal of Inclusive Education*, **2**(4), pp. 359–69.

Maclagan, I. (2002) 'Making rights stick: Children's Rights Commission work in Oxfordshire', *Support for Learning*, **17**(3), pp. 133–7.

Mason, M. (1992) 'Internalised oppression' in Rieser, R. and Mason, M. *Disability Equality in the Classroom: a human rights issue*, London, Disability Equality in Education.

Nixon, J., Allan, J. and Mannion, G. (2001) 'Educational renewal as democratic practice: 'new' community schooling in Scotland', *International Journal of Inclusive Education*, **5**(4), pp. 329–52.

Penrose, V., Thomas, G., and Greed, C. (2001) 'Designing inclusive schools: how can children be involved?', *Support for Learning*, **16**(2), pp. 87–91.

Quicke, J. (2003) 'Educating the pupil voice', *Support for Learning*, **18**(2), pp. 51–7.

Ramrayka, L. (2003) 'Sure strategy', *The Guardian* (Guardian Extra, p. 2), 25 June 2003.

Rieser, R. (1992) 'Internalised oppression: how it seems to me' in Rieser, R. and Mason, M. *Disability Equality in the Classroom: a human rights issue*, London, Disability Equality in Education.

Searle, C. (2001) *An Exclusive Education: race, class and exclusion in British schools*, London, Lawrence and Wishart.

Scottish Executive (2002) New Community Schools website. Available from: http://www.scotland.gov.uk/education/ newcommunityschools/default.htm (accessed April 8, 2002).

Scottish Office (1998) 'New Community Schools Prospectus' [online], Scottish Office. Available from: http://www.scotland.gov.uk/library/ documents-w3/ncsp-03.htm (accessed January 31, 2004).

Slee, R. (1999) 'Policies and practices? Inclusive education and its effects on schooling' in Daniels, H. and Garner, P. *Inclusive Education*, London, Kogan Page.

Tunstill, J., Allnock, D., Meadows, P. and McLeod, A. (2002) 'Early experiences of implementing Sure Start' [online], Birkbeck, University of London. Available from: http://www.ness.bbk.ac.uk (accessed September 21, 2003).

Whalley, M. (1994) *Learning to be Strong: setting up a neighbourhood service for under-fives and their families*, London, Hodder and Stoughton.

Wolfendale, S. (1985) 'Overview of parental participation in children's education' in Topping, K. and Wolfendale, S. (eds) *Parental Involvement in Children's Reading*, London, Croom Helm.

Wolfendale, S. (ed.) (2000) *Special Needs in the Early Years: snapshots of practice*, London, Routledge Falmer.

UNIT 10   Changing places

Prepared for the course team by Kieron Sheehy

Contents

1   Introduction

This unit looks at a range of provision that exists within the UK for children with 'low incidence disabilities' (DfEE, 1997). These are pupils that the Government recognized in its vision of *Excellence for all Children* as having the most 'severe and complex difficulties' and as continuing 'to need specialist support' (DfEE, 1997, p. 53). 'Low incidence' refers to the fact that there are not many children with these impairments per LEA.

Because of relatively low numbers, LEAs may decide to group these children in particular schools or areas to target resources in the most efficient way. For the children and parents themselves there might be issues of contact with other young people with similar experiences. Often these children do not attend their local schools, or are segregated or included on the basis of a diagnosis or identification of need such as visual or hearing impairment or profound autistic spectrum disorder. LEAs are expected to make regional arrangements to co-operate to ensure 'specialised in-service teacher training' and support services for these children (DfEE, 1997, p. 55).

Unit 10 provides examples of the different kinds of provision for children with low incidence disabilities and critically analyses the provision in terms of concepts developed throughout the course, for example, human rights, the social model of disability, curriculum responses to learning difficulties and discourses within education. The unit considers factors operating within such provision and some of the ways in which these factors can work towards or impede the development of inclusive education.

Learning outcomes

By the end of this unit you will have:

- developed your own position regarding the presence of a diverse range of provision for children and young people with 'low incidence disabilities';
- considered the appropriateness of such provision from your own and others' perspectives;
- debated whether such provision is developing inclusion or reconstructing barriers to inclusion.

Resources for this unit

For this unit you will need:

- Video Band C, 'Changing places'
- Chapter 8, Reader 2, 'Autism in special and inclusive schools: "there has to be a point to their being there"' by Priscilla Alderson and Christopher Goodey.

2 Diversity of provision

In any period of time we can find children experiencing different types of education in a variety of different settings across the UK. Jennifer Evans and Ingrid Lunt surveyed LEAs in England and Wales in 2002. The LEAs in their sample gave the following examples of the various forms of 'currently practised inclusion' (Evans and Lunt, 2002). The percentages refer to the number of LEAs in the survey who used each type of provision. It was common for LEAs to use a mixture of forms.

1   Part-time placements in special and in mainstream schools. (78 per cent)

2   Outreach support from special school to integrated pupils. (60 per cent)

3   Units or centres on the site of a mainstream school. (92 per cent)

4   Modifications to mainstream facilities. (76 per cent)

5   Additionally resourced mainstream schools. (80 per cent)

6   Supported placements in mainstream schools. (96 per cent)

In this unit we look at options 1, 2, 3 and 5 of this list, concentrating on 3 and 5, and discuss whether we would construct them as examples of inclusion in action.

Children with quite different learning difficulties or impairments experience this range of specialized provision. For example, children with a visual impairment (VI) may be taught in several of the settings listed above. A Royal National Institute for the Blind survey of 22,000 children with visual impairments, aged two to sixteen, in LEAs across the UK found the following variety of educational environments:

1   36 per cent of VI children have multiple disabilities and are supported by LEA visual impairment services.

2   60 per cent of VI children aged 5 to 16 are educated in mainstream schools, including those who are additionally resourced for VI (64.5 per cent of primary aged VI children and 55.5 per cent of secondary school children with a visual impairment attend mainstream/resourced mainstream schools).

3   7 per cent of VI children are educated in special schools for visual impairment (5 per cent of primary aged VI children and 10 per cent of secondary school children with a visual impairment attend VI special schools).

4   31 per cent of VI children attend other types of special schools.

5   2 per cent of VI children and those who have multiple disabilities combined with a visual impairment (MDVI) are

educated elsewhere, e.g. independent schools, hospital schools or at home.

(Miller, 2002, pp. 67–8)

This survey shows that there is a clustering of visually impaired children, at least in the primary phase, in resourced schools, that is, schools given additional resources, usually for an identified group of children. The majority of visually impaired children attend mainstream schools and there is a trend within LEAs away from *separate* specialist provision.

The range of provision for visually impaired children recorded by Miller reflects the school placements of other children with low incidence 'needs' or impairments. For example, children with severe learning difficulties (SLD) and profound and multiple learning difficulties (PMLD) experience a similar diversity of educational placements. Penny Lacey's (2001) survey of sixty schools found that children might be:

a) in a special school with one or more sessions per week in mainstream;

b) in a special school with mainstream pupils joining them for special lessons;

c) on the roll of the special school but attending mainstream part-time;

d) in a special class/unit/school within a mainstream school with one or more session per week in mainstream;

e) in a resourced mainstream school and withdrawn for specialist input;

f) in a mainstream school full-time.

(Lacey, 2001, p. 160)

Some children with PMLD were taught in units within special schools and joined in with the rest of the school for varying activities and proportions of time.

Before we go on to look at some of these educational placements in detail, you might like to reflect on this range of provision. Do you think it represents a necessary diversity? Or does it suggest that inclusion is a 'postcode lottery', that a person's experience will be determined by where s/he lives and by historical traditions rather than by choice or suitability? The examples and discussions in this unit will help you to develop and analyse your initial thoughts on this matter.

One way in which we can examine our beliefs concerning the diversity of provision for children with low incidence disabilities is by reflecting on what we would consider to be ideal. Margaret Hardman and Julie Worthington (2000) collected views from educational psychologists about the kind of placement they saw as ideal for children with particular 'types of special need'. These are illustrated in Table 1.

Table 1   Hypothetical ideal placements (percentages)

Type of special need	Special school	Mainstream unit	Mainstream with support	Mainstream
Profound/multiple learning difficulties	82	16	2	0
Severe learning difficulties	28	38	33	1
Moderate learning difficulties	6	22	67	5
Mild learning difficulties	3	31	49	17
Specific (dyslexia)	0	4	65	31
Emotional and behavioural difficulties	5	23	56	16
Physical difficulties	5	17	75	3
Hearing impaired	4	55	37	4
Visually impaired	11	44	44	1
Speech and language difficulties	1	26	53	20
Medical conditions	7	19	55	19
Total (% placements)	13	29	48	10

(Hardman and Worthington, 2000, p. 353)

Activity 10.1

What would be your ideal? Would you place all children within mainstream schools or would you make a link between a labelled category and a particular placement? Your responses here will reflect the way in which you interpret and respond to particular categories and, indeed, to the idea of categories altogether (see Units 1 and 2).

Do you see the segregation of any group from mainstream schools in your ideal? Record your main thoughts regarding different provision for different groups in your learning journal. We will revisit this issue at the end of the unit so that you can see if and how your position has changed.

How you respond to the diversity of provision depends on the perspectives and beliefs that you have developed so far. For example, we are unlikely to welcome the same patterns of provision when we regard a child as the victim of personal tragedy compared to when we regard that child as disabled by the social consequences of her impairment.

Opinions that others have given about this include the following:

- Inclusion, in the UK, has not been implemented overnight. Inclusion is constructed as a journey and diversity is a necessary, but temporary, 'step along the way'. Different schools and LEAs are moving at different rates.
- Diversity of provision represents the limits of inclusion, that is, there are always some children who are not, and will never be, suited for education with their peers, or at least full-time education with their peers (e.g., Shanker, 1995).
- Diversity is essential and shows a positive cultural choice. For example, members of the Deaf community would argue from this viewpoint (Jarvis *et al.*, Chapter 18, Reader 1). This idea of diversity might extend to 'faith schools' for other communities of learners.
- The range of provision suggests a denial of human rights. The range does not indicate choices that people have made but rather 'where they have been put' by others (e.g. Mittler, 2000).
- It is economically and pragmatically sensible to group children with low incidence 'needs' together (e.g. DfEE, 1997). Diversity reveals a diversity of funding arrangements and relative wealth.

So far we have identified the variety of educational provision for children with low incidence disabilities and you have begun to consider your attitude to this diversity. We now go on to look at specific examples of such provision.

3 Units within mainstream schools

Units or centres on the sites of mainstream schools are increasingly common. In the next activity you will view video material about Archers Court School and Aspen 2, a secondary school with a resource base for a particular group of children. You will also see excerpts about Willingdon, a primary school with a facility for hearing-impaired children. We then go on to consider a unit for children with autism. You will be exploring these examples with the core course aim of developing perspectives on inclusive education in mind. There are many ways in which one might consider the selected examples in relation to inclusion. We would like you to think about some of these *before* you watch the video.

A period of transition?

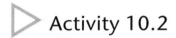 Activity 10.2

First, construct a table of factors and questions that you think are important in assessing how inclusive a particular educational setting is. These may include possible sources of exclusion. You will use these factors and questions to structure and record your observations about Aspen 2 and Willingdon. This is essential preparation for TMA 03.

The sample table that follows shows some possible factors and questions. While it may include some of these, your table will of course be different, reflecting your own views and priorities. The third, blank column is for your observations and any further questions you would want to ask after watching the video, including any questions in your table that the video material did not provide answers to.

Table 2   Factors and questions in assessing inclusion

Factor	Questions	Observations and further questions
Name	Do some pupils attend something that has a different name to the rest of the school?	
Physical location	Are they actually in the school physically?	
Funding	Are they part of the school's budget?	
Pattern of attendance	Is some form of selection used to determine who attends the school?	
Registration	Are all pupils part of ordinary class registration?	
The curriculum/ curriculum arrangements	Do all pupils follow the same curriculum? Do they differentiate and in what ways?	
History	Is this an 'advance' from a previous system? Which groups might see this as an improvement?	
Planned future	Is this a step along the way or seen as an end point?	
The view of inclusion presented	How do people talk about inclusion? Are there official and unofficial views?	
Pupils' views	Are the pupils consulted in the running of the school?	
Social inclusion	What are the patterns of mixing and social interaction?	

Now watch Video Band C, parts 1 and 2, 'Changing places' and complete your table by filling in the 'observations and further questions' column.

 By recording your observations you will have established your own view about the degree to which Aspen 2 and Willingdon represent inclusive education or are a move towards inclusive education. You will probably have identified some contradictions and tensions, for example, with regard to issues of physical access or the discourses used by pupils and teachers in discussing the school. Young people may be described as 'Aspen children' rather than Archers Court pupils. Obviously these discourses have implications for how pupils are expected to engage with the curriculum and school life in general. You may have noted examples of this. You will also have seen several types of differentiation and support being used across a variety of subject lessons and you may have reflected on this in light of our discussions in Unit 8.

Alistair, the head of Aspen 2, is clearly aware of the potential to 'recreate a special school within a mainstream school'. He suggests that although the physical movement of Aspen 2 from its temporary site into the main school building may minimize this, the major difference (from being a special school) is the degree of social inclusion that occurs.

• •

The attitudes of all members of a school are an essential factor in enabling a movement towards inclusion or in stalling, or subverting, such attempts. Evelyn McGregor and Elaine Campbell (2001) asked teachers in Scotland about their attitudes towards having children with autism in mainstream schools. They found that special school teachers of children with autism, unlike mainstream teachers, highlighted teacher attitudes as being vital for 'successful integration'. Further, mainstream teachers who had taught children with autism were much more likely to express positive attitudes, irrespective of whether they had received specialist training or not. However, only 'a minority of mainstream respondents believed children with autism should be integrated where possible' (McGregor and Campbell, 2001, p. 189). (This study used the term integration rather than inclusion.)

The next reading looks at aspects of attitudes and practices within two different educational settings for children with autism.

An end point?

◯ Activity 10.3

Now read Chapter 8 in Reader 2, 'Autism in special and inclusive schools: "there has to be a point to their being there"' by Priscilla Alderson and Christopher Goodey.

Alderson and Goodey describe a unit on the site of a mainstream school and make a comparison with an inclusive setting. In doing so they raise the question of why a separate unit might exist for these children. The authors conclude that it is often very difficult to 'diagnose' and identify any educational difficulties that are unique to the children within the unit. Would you agree, therefore, that this undermines the case for separate units, or are there important points that the authors have not considered? Could you identify positive features of the unit that do not exist within the inclusive setting?

Therapy

For many children and young people with low incidence disabilities, such as speech and communication difficulties or profound and multiple learning difficulties, therapy, such as speech and language therapy or physiotherapy, is a necessary part of their *educational* lives. Limited ideas about how a therapy service can be offered can form a barrier to inclusion. Children and parents may be given the choice of a special school with paramedical or therapeutic support or a mainstream placement with very little. As one parent noted, 'I was told I couldn't have my cake and eat it' (Mackey and McQueen, 1998, p. 22).

Sue Mackey and Jill McQueen (1998) found that most teachers and parents would have preferred physiotherapy to occur within the school. Moreover, 84 per cent of children that they contacted said that the 'split' between physical education and physiotherapy was the most difficult thing they experienced regarding inclusion. Mackey and McQueen concluded that professionals need to share and develop new practices in order to work for the child rather than fitting the child in to existing models of professional practice, for example in which physiotherapy only occurs in hospitals. As John O'Brien concludes, 'segregation takes care of itself, collaboration takes work' (O'Brien cited in Mackey and McQueen, 1998).

You may have considered how the therapy aspect of inclusion was managed in Aspen 2. Alistair, the head, had this to say:

Therapy, whatever particular nature, takes place at the moment in our therapy room. Now because we're in temporary accommodation at the moment, that facility is quite small. Moving into purpose-built accommodation within the next year or so will be a suite of therapy rooms for physiotherapy, occupational therapy, multi-sensory work, music therapy. So we'll be able to deliver a programme which will be as good as, and as effective as, any special school.

(E243 Video, Band C, pages 408–10)

You will recall that Norman Kunc presented a critical view of 'therapies' in Unit 7, giving his perspective as a 'user'.

We have considered two examples of separate units on the sites of mainstream schools: Aspen 2, a unit for children with severe and profound learning difficulties whose staff see it as part of a movement towards inclusion, and, in Alderson and Goodey, a unit for children with autistic spectrum disorder which appears to see itself as separated provision, an end point in terms of the 'limits' of inclusion. The two examples present different beliefs and practices about themselves and their pupils.

We have raised the importance of attitudes, rather than just physical location, as a key factor in moving towards inclusion. In the next section we look at additionally resourced mainstream schools, with a focus on the interpersonal and social aspects of such provision.

Additionally resourced mainstream schools

Additionally resourced mainstream schools are those in which additional resources have been targeted, usually for a particular group of pupils. For example, a school might be resourced with teachers of the Deaf and sign language interpreters, as in Willingdon school (although in that case the funding arrangements are separated between the hearing-impaired facility and the rest of the school).

Pat Cuckle and June Wilson (2002) give a description of a typical 'resourced school'. There were bases where children registered at the start of the morning and from where they left in the afternoon. Pupils joined mainstream lessons across the curriculum and ate lunch with their mainstream peers. Access to a resourced school place was, however, variable. For example, in the large metropolitan LEA that Cuckle and Wilson looked at, 83 per cent of pupils with Down syndrome were in mainstream schools at primary level (17 per cent in special schools). However, at secondary level only 12 per cent remained in mainstream, while 33 per cent had moved to resourced provision and 54 per cent had transferred to special schools.

Social experiences

Cuckle and Wilson (2002) went beyond the statistics to investigate the social experiences of pupils with Down syndrome.

> In terms of social relationships and friendships, resourced provision within a mainstream setting has the potential to provide age-appropriate role models as well as access to other young people with special needs and social interests. The resourced provision contrasts with mainstream high school settings where there may be very few or no other young people with quite the same needs.
>
> *(Cuckle and Wilson, 2002, p. 66)*

Cuckle and Wilson suggest that resourced provision enables children both to pick up 'appropriate' social behaviour and to 'have access to friends with similar needs, and whose levels of maturity and interests may be more evenly matched to their own' (p. 70). They conclude:

> Young people with Down's syndrome evidently enjoyed and benefited from having role-models among and experiencing such relationships and friendships with mainstream peers; however, such relationships were largely confined to school. More truly reciprocal relationships and friendships seemed to exist between them and other young people with special needs (including those with Down's syndrome) whose interests, social life, emotional maturity and communication skills were more equally matched. There are obvious advantages for young people experiencing both groups of friends.
>
> *(Cuckle and Wilson, 2002, p. 71)*

Activity 10.4

What do you think of Cuckle and Wilson's rationale? Are all children positioned equally in this view? Jot down your initial thoughts on the above paragraph.

 On first reading, these observations and conclusions may seem to be common sense and unproblematic. On further reading and reflection, however, you may identify some ways in which opinions implicit here do not fit with some rights or inclusion positions. We noted the following points of concern.

- There seems to be a split between pupils who are 'role models' and pupils who have 'special needs'; the two are regarded as distinct and separate groups. Why can't 'pupils with special needs' be role models too? Don't some 'mainstream' pupils make poor role models?

- There is a danger of perceiving the disabled pupils largely as receivers of support, guidance, friendly overtures and not as actively shaping social dynamics. If the friendships across disabled/non-disabled pupils are not reciprocal, why might this be? What are the barriers to the pupils mixing outside of school and developing their friendships further? Rannveig Traustadottir (2000) argues that the nature of the friendships between disabled and non-disabled people are more complex than many of the over-romanticized notions frequently portrayed.
- If friendships between pupils who have more matched interests, maturity levels and communications skills are more reciprocal, why is it that the social mixing of disabled people with non-disabled people is so aspired to? Anne Louise Chappell (1994) argues that an implicit message in the normalization ideology has been that mixing with 'ordinary' people rather than other people with learning difficulties brings greater status and greater worth. If this underpins any desire for inclusive placements there is a mixed message emerging about valuing diversity.

There are debates about who is benefiting in what ways from resourced provision. For example, if research suggests that deaf students gain academic advantages in attending resourced programmes but some social advantages in attending segregated settings (van Gurp, 2001), this might lead to a 'which is best' discussion. This can be seen as detracting from the central issue that the disabled pupils have a fundamental right to be in the schools. The tension, though, arises from whether their right is to a place in their local school or in one with some specialized input. Think back to the Willingdon section of the video. Neither Natasha nor Megan attended their original local school. One implication of this is that their local schools may not develop their potential to become inclusive; channelling resources and expertise into a few schools may undermine the inclusivity of the majority.

Activity 10.5

A local school for local people assumes that a certain type of community exists or is desirable. How well does this idea match up with other aspects of one's life?

Consider the area in which you live. Of the services, organizations and events that you use, which are local and which are not?

Draw a diagram or picture to show the geographical 'spread' of these aspects of your life. The two diagrams in Figure 10.1 provide contrasting examples.

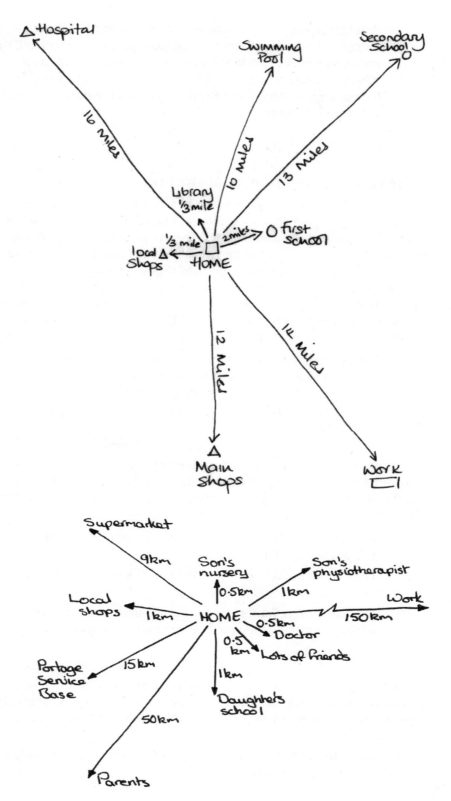

Figure 10.1   The geographical spread of lives.

What factors do you think determine the location of these aspects? Reflect on how important 'being local' is to you and the extent to which this might influence your position about local schools. As you do this, think back to the video of Pen Green and Bannockburn (Video Band B) and what those two facilities meant to their local communities.

· ·

The resource of additional staffing

Children within resourced schools may still have support assistants or teachers working primarily with them. Indeed, this is often a key part of a school being seen as resourced. The presence of support staff can be based on a particular child's 'needs'. In your analysis of Aspen 2 and Willingdon you may have decided that how support staff work within a school was one criterion for juding how inclusive the school was. Investigating good practice in teaching deaf children within mainstream schools, Steve Powers (2001) found the ways in which staff work were important.

> The deaf pupil can view the support teacher as 'baggage' that the young person has to drag round from lesson to lesson. The effect of the extra helper on the pupil's attitude to learning can be to reduce pupil motivation and initiative.
>
> *(Powers, 2001, p. 188)*

The way in which the children perceive any support they receive is therefore an important part of inclusion. Tony Bowers (1997) found that children gave a range of explanations of why support staff were in a classroom:

> 'Because some children are slow learners and they have a special teacher' (Girl: 9 years)
>
> 'They are doing different jobs because the other teacher is for special needs' (Boy: 13 years)
>
> 'Because if there was only one teacher all their attention would go on the people who have disabilities' (Boy: 13 years)
>
> *(Bowers, 1997, p. 225)*

So, one might see situations where support aimed at promoting inclusion can recreate barriers to inclusion, clearly re-establishing the special within the mainstream. Do you think this situation can be avoided?

Steve Powers found several examples in which deaf pupils negotiated the level and type of support they received.

In one service the secondary pupils have a say in their own support programmes. They can negotiate the amount of support they receive and, up to a point, the subject(s) they omit from the curriculum in order to receive support – they can elect to have 'support' as one of their curricular options. Support teachers and the class teachers rely heavily on the comments and feedback offered by pupils. Pupils are encouraged to take responsibility for their own learning needs from as early an age as possible.

(Powers, 2001, pp. 186–7)

Do you think that this would address some of the problems implied by the pupils' ideas about in-class support quoted above? (You will have seen examples of pupils and learning support assistants working together in the video.) Penny Lacey (2001) considered this aspect of school life for pupils with severe and profound learning difficulties:

Child A (from the special school) was wheeled into the playground by the LSA [learning support assistant].

Child B (from the mainstream school) asked the LSA if she could play with Child A. The LSA suggested that Child B should ask Child A herself and then walked away from the pair so that they could interact without her. Child A and Child B were observed talking together and with other children.

Here the LSA seemed very clear that her role was to enable children to talk and play together with the minimum of support from her. Another example further illustrates her support style ...

The LSA supported two pupils with SLD [in an art class]. She sat between the two pupils and they all sat opposite three pupils from the mainstream class. The conversation was focused on the art for some of the time and on social things for the rest. The LSA asked questions to start the conversation then she was quiet while the pupils talked to each other. When the communication broke down, as it often did through the poor articulation or restricted understanding of the pupils with SLD, the LSA intervened and interpreted or simplified the language.

(Lacey, 2001, pp. 161–2)

By giving these examples we are arguing that the skills of the LSA or learning supporter are essential in determining the degree to which resourced support of pupils becomes inclusive. This is an ongoing and dynamic process happening between people.

This is highlighted in the Willingdon examples seen on the video. The LSAs have to make complex and demanding decisions on a moment-

An LSA supports a hearing-impaired child at Willingdon Primary School.

by-moment basis. The three choices they have are explained in Table 3.

Table 3   A comparison of British Sign Language and two sign systems

British Sign Language (BSL)	*Signed supported English (SSE)*	*Signed English (SE)*
BSL is recognised as a language distinct from English. It is the sign language indigenous to the deaf community of Britain. It has been defined as a visual, gestural language in terms of both its perception and production. As it is perceived visually within space, signs can be combined simultaneously to convey meaning. Body and head posture, facial expression and lip movements all play a distinctive role in contributing to meaning.	This is a manual support system incorporating signs taken from BSL together with fingerspelling. It is used in English word order to supplement spoken words but does not attempt to present every element of the spoken utterance. Its aim is to clarify the spoken message and lessen ambiguity.	Signs taken from BSL together with generated signs and markers, are used, with fingerspelling to give an exact manual representation of spoken English. It is used primarily as a tool for the teaching of reading and writing.

(BATOD, 2003)

The Willingdon LSAs need to resolve the tension between the language demands of BSL, the school curriculum and the children's home background. As Mary, a Willingdon LSA notes, these are often in conflict:

> I have a choice of three ... I can use with the children. All based on signing ... pure BSL and sign supported English and pure signed English. Most of the time I use sign supported English because at the moment I'm working with children who don't use BSL at home and so they are quite at home with the word order.
>
> ... If I had a child who used BSL at home I would veer far more to the BSL side. But the only time I'd use pure signed English is in a literacy lesson when we're concerned with the endings on words and the words that are in-between. There's no time to do that anyway in normal speaking speed. You could never do it.
>
> *(Video Band C, pages 432–5)*

With children with hearing impairments grouped together in the resourced school, such decisions are made more complex by the range of children's need. In a local school there might be just one pupil needing sign support. The fact that the children are clustered in this way, though, means that they have each other as well as hearing children as communication partners and language learning resources. Such clustering of children makes economic sense in terms of targeting resources. Teachers of the Deaf and sign language interpreters are not readily available, but, again, this says something about society's values.

Identity as a resource

School staff bring their own identities and cultures to a school and this also influences the degree to which a resourced school is inclusive. Clear messages about disability – who we value and what we see as possible – are given to children by the type of people who hold positions of responsibility within schools and how these people are treated. Teachers with impairments can be the best resource a school can have, but this is not always recognized.

> **Blind teacher made to feel a 'burden' wins discrimination case**
>
> *Tuesday 4 July 2000*
>
> The Association of Teachers and Lecturers (ATL) has won a significant disability discrimination and unfair, constructive dismissal case for Liz Abbott, a teacher who is registered blind, against her former employers, St Mary's Roman Catholic Primary School in Chingford, East London. The tribunal summed up by saying that ' ... Mrs

Abbott had become a burden to ... *[her employers]* and one they no longer wished to bear'.

Speaking at a press conference held today ... in London, Sharon Liburd, ATL solicitor, described how the school employed Liz Abbott, an experienced and dedicated teacher who needed an assistant to carry out her duties as a classroom teacher. However, when the assistant left, very little or no attempt was made by the school to recruit a replacement, the main reason given being budgetary restraints. Mrs Abbott was left with the task of investigating ways to fund an assistant and even when she presented a paper outlining all the available schemes, her employers did not pursue the matter further. Ms Liburd explained how Mrs Abbott felt her employers treated her as though she was a problem and a burden. Mrs Abbott retired on ill health grounds in 1997.

The tribunal hearing in Stratford, East London found the school had breached the Disability Discrimination Act 1995 and the Employment Rights Act 1996. It concluded that the school had failed to ensure that Mrs Abbott was provided with 'reasonable adjustments' so that she could perform her job as a classroom teacher and that she was unfairly dismissed. Under the terms of an undisclosed settlement, Mrs Abbott received a substantial sum for loss of earnings and injury to feelings.

Commenting on her experience, Liz Abbott said:

> When a statement is made about you being a burden, it makes you feel like a second class citizen. Nobody deserves this kind of treatment. It took the decision of an impartial tribunal to prove to me that this whole experience was not my fault. I was beginning to doubt my own abilities not only as a teacher but as a person.

> If the Disability Discrimination Act can stop others being put in this position, and if it can become a source of support for those who are put in this position, then it's got to be working.

Sharon Liburd, ATL solicitor, said:

> The school failed to take reasonable action to ensure that Mrs Abbott could function as a classroom teacher and the local authority failed to honour its equal opportunities policy.

> Funding for the assistant's post had been received during the preceding eight years. There was no logical reason for the school to think that funding would not be available for a new classroom assistant.

Mrs Abbott felt extremely let down by those who ought to have known better.

(Association of Teachers and Lecturers, 2000)

While the example of Mrs Abbott is not necessarily about a resourced school, it highlights the interaction between human resources and attitudes. The way in which this is managed is vital to all places of learning that wish to become more inclusive. G. Denise Lance describes her experience as a lecturer in a 'virtual classroom'.

> When I accepted a job teaching a course on inclusion for general educators, I faced a dilemma associated with the anonymity of online communication. The purpose of the class was to make general educators more comfortable with teaching students with disabilities. Would my disability help create positive attitudes about individuals with disabilities, create negative attitudes, or have no effect at all?
>
> I felt strongly that my experiences as a student with cerebral palsy [CP] in general education was important to share, as part of my expertise on inclusion. However, I wanted my students to begin the course examining their concerns about teaching students with disabilities. I feared that my disclosing my disability at the onset might temper the teachers' real anxieties and that they might not be as forthcoming, fearing that they would offend their instructor.
>
> For my first time teaching the course, I waited until the fourth week of class, when our topics included physical and multiple disabilities, to disclose my having cerebral palsy. To integrate my experiences as smoothly into the course as possible, I thought of myself as a guest speaker in my own class. Each week, I posted several questions to which students responded through a threaded discussion. One of the questions for Week Four appeared as follows:
>
>> What would you ask a student with CP who was included during her entire educational career? Post your questions to the discussion board, and I will answer. I was an included student with CP and learned a great deal from the experience. I have difficulty using my hands, walking, and speaking. I type with my feet. I waited until now to tell you this because I did not want you to censor your feelings about teaching students with disabilities or be afraid you might hurt my feelings. But now that you know, I would be happy to answer any questions you may have about being an included student with a significant disability!
>
> *(Lance, 2002)*

The benefits to students of having a disabled teacher go beyond the first-hand experience and professional knowledge that they bring.

> *'Lister Community School* is resourced for deaf students', says Jill Kirk, teacher for the Deaf at Lister School. 'Many of the deaf students and their hearing peers come from a feeder primary school. We already had those links and deaf students would move across with hearing peers who could already sign, they were quite used to having deaf students in their class. So, the hearing pupils are quite deaf-aware already. It is really important we don't ignore the whole thing around deaf culture and deaf community. Also, we couldn't run this type of provision if we didn't employ deaf adults as we do. That's really important for deaf identity.'
>
> *(Channel 4, 2002)*

We suggest that an indicator of a school moving towards inclusion is the presence of disabled staff as well as students. And while this might be seen as an *essential* resource in an additionally resourced school, fewer barriers to teaching for disabled people and therefore more disabled teachers throughout the entire system would impact on the 'need' for such 'special' schools.

It is interesting to pose the question of whether we might need additionally resourced schools for disabled teachers. This might lead us into the issue of rights to employment. A disabled teacher should not be discriminated against and have the choice of school in which s/he can teach limited by the resources available. If this is a convincing argument, however (and we believe it is), where does it leave resourced schools for pupils? From this perspective, they are a response to a lack of equal opportunities as much as a means of enhancing access. Is the answer to additionally resource some mainstream schools or to tackle the equal opportunity issue more radically?

5 From special schools to inclusive service: an inclusive trajectory or going nowhere fast?

One of the factors that you may have considered in your analysis of Aspen 2 in Activity 10.2 was its future aspirations and plans. To look at where a school is at one point in time does not give us the full picture.

One might suggest that the plans held by a school and the future *envisioned* by its members are important factors in the extent to which we see it as inclusive. This goal will affect the way that people interact in the here and now.

Aspen 2: the temporary separate site.

A child from Aspen 2 joins the mainstream.

In this section we examine the process of change and consider examples where special provision has developed to become more inclusive. As we have mentioned, a 'vision' is important, but there are other factors that facilitate this process and without which change would remain a dream. Can you identify these factors in the following example of the transformation of a special school?

The Somerset story

An example of a change in practice that has clearly developed towards inclusion is that of the Princess Margaret School in Taunton, Somerset. This was founded in 1966 as a Barnardos special day and boarding school for children with physical disabilities.

Carol Bannister and colleagues describe how the school gradually transformed itself and its working practices in order to promote the inclusion of its pupils. (You can, if you wish to follow this up, read about this transition in Chapter 10 in Reader 2, 'Changing from a special school to an inclusion service' by Bannister *et al.*) Here we give a summary, using subheadings to highlight how we saw this process of change.

A belief

The starting point for this change was the belief that 'inclusion is right and segregation is wrong'. The school was seen as having considerable strength and expertise in its work as a special school. Interestingly, being a successful school was raised by staff as a potential barrier to change.

A purpose

The school's purpose and 'mission' was reconsidered and stated as including 'empowering pupils, developing services and influencing the wider environment'.

Supporting something new

In 1992 an advisory teacher was appointed (jointly between Barnardos and Somerset LEA) to support an integration scheme, helping children fit into mainstream schools and supporting them within these.

A change

In 1994 a teacher within the school proposed that her entire class should transfer to a local primary. This included the transfer of herself, classroom assistants, speech therapist and physiotherapist as well as the children. Subsequently other year groups transferred in different ways.

A wider influence

Two years later the school closed and in its place was a project at the core of the Somerset Inclusion Service. The change was reported positively in the local press:

> Barnardos Princess Margaret Special School in Taunton, Somerset, closes after 30 years. The pupils are moving to six primary and two secondary schools in the county with Barnardos offering special support. Each pupil will have a designated classroom assistant and Barnardos will provide physiotherapy and speech and language therapy on the school sites. A teacher co-ordinator will ensure tailoring of the curriculum to each child's needs. Toby Mildon, aged 15, who has already moved to mainstream, said his advice to other young people would be: 'Just get out there and do it. They may think it's going to be really hard, that they are going to be separate, that they are going to stick out. But I don't think it's like that at all. Society has got a lot better at dealing with disability.'

> *(CSIE, 1996)*

A feature of the new service was the teacher co-ordinators, who were the former special school staff, managing the inclusion of children whom they had previously taught. From one special school initiative came more inclusive local schools and, in 1997, a 'support service network':

> The centrally managed team of teachers and support assistants work closely with health services, social services and the voluntary sector to provide specialist, in-depth support by means of advice, direct teaching and personal care. We aim to provide a planned pattern of mainstream provision across the County for both physical and curriculum access. We will develop multi-professional working alongside other support services and cascade specialist training packages to pupils, teachers and parents.

> *(Somerset County Council, no date)*

While this example is of schools in transition, it also illustrates the potential shortcomings of resourced-style provision. Six months after the positive press report quoted above, another local newspaper reported on one family who were unhappy with the resourced school model.

> The parents of Jacob Smith, one of many pupils being integrated from Barnardos Princess Margaret School, Taunton, say that Somerset Education Authority has let them down. Angie and Marcus Smith want Jacob, who has cerebral palsy, to go to his local secondary school but the LEA say he must travel to a school which has been especially adapted for disabled pupils. Somerset's deputy education officer, John Rose, said: 'We have put up £200,000 in the past year to adapt schools and it is an on-going programme but we can't do every school because we do not have the resources'.
>
> *(CSIE, 1997)*

What would your response to Jacob and his parents be in this situation? Do you find yourself adopting the family's rights position – that Jacob has a moral right to attend his local school – or the LEA's position that they have a duty to use resources efficiently? Does this individual story alter the way we might see Somerset's inclusion service as an inclusive model or as a transition to an inclusive model? Or might it be viewed as a pragmatic compromise that is more like a cul-de-sac than a through road to greater inclusion?

The lessons of the Somerset project include:

- inclusive ideals may not be held by everyone and require much discussion;
- there is a need to write down the purpose and educational philosophy clearly and make it widely available;
- all stakeholders (parents, students, the LEA, local mainstream schools) need to be involved;
- it is worth establishing a 'futures' group to determine ways of bringing about change and a timetable for change;
- not all children and staff will want to be part of the inclusive alternative to special schools.

These reflections give us some insights into what this particular journey was like for the people involved. Their project demanded a great deal of collaboration and considerable vision. It serves as a useful example of the issues people face at key times in the transition to inclusion. It is likely that future pupils will have a more inclusive set-up, but did the pupils during the transition suffer on their behalf? Were they subject to uncertainty, shifting expectations and anxieties that were unfair on them? Can we say that this is necessary for the greater good when this is a real issue for the children and parents caught up in transitions?

A London journey: beyond resourced schools

Unless we adopt wholesale, overnight change, there will inevitably be compromises in terms of inclusion. In 1984 the London Borough of Newham, which you may recall from Unit 5, became one of the first in the UK to instigate a transition towards inclusive education. They had a clear 'mission statement':

> The ultimate goal of Newham's Inclusive Education policy is to make it possible for every child, whatever special educational needs they may have, to attend their neighbourhood school, and to have full access to the curriculum and to be able to participate in every aspect of mainstream life and achieve their full potential.
>
> *(Newham Council cited in Jordan and Goodey, 1996, p. 8)*

Newham faced the task of getting this vision shared by over 100,000 people in the borough's education system. They began this process using resourced schools. In *Human Rights and School Change: the Newham story* Linda Jordan and Chris Goodey describe the way Newham changed their system and acknowledge that the setting up of resourced schools was very much a compromise.

> Parents of some of the children attending special schools simply would not have allowed their children to have gone to the local school. This is especially true for parents of autistic children and children with multiple disabilities.
>
> *(Jordan and Goodey, 1996, p. 10)*

This was a new venture and parents and schools needed to develop confidence in this new way of working. The resourced school idea seemed to meet this need, although it maintained a 'labels and conditions' approach (see Unit 2). Changes did not happen overnight and parents in favour of inclusion had to battle for resources that we might regard as basic rights.

Interestingly, disabled adults within Newham were able to inform and influence the process of educational change through consultative committees. This was important in addressing and finding solutions to problems that arose. For example, there were differences of opinion in the deaf community about whether mainstream placement would destroy deaf culture. Also, parents were concerned about the loss of the expertise of teachers from the special schools. The resourced school model emerged from these discussions as the favoured option (Jordan and Goodey, 1996), with a primary and secondary school being resourced. When the existing special school for the Deaf finally closed in 1992 a new service began. This operated from a bilingual ethos and the borough employed communicators, interpreters and deaf adults to work in mainstream classes.

Changes such as this take a large amount of goodwill, hard work and consistent commitment from a lot of different people. Jordan and Goodey describe the effort and belief that went into this transformation and show that it was by no means a smooth process.

> The basic principles could easily have got lost in the confusion, anger and passion that was generated. By reminding everyone that there was a plan to end segregation because of the human rights of children and young people, it was somehow always just possible to gain some level of agreement about the way forward.
>
> *(Jordan and Goodey, 1996, p. 25)*

So, how far has this process got? In 1984 there were 711 pupils in eight special schools plus three separate classes, and 202 attending out-of-borough special schools. By 1996 there were 99 pupils at the two remaining special schools and approximately 99 out of borough, plus a third special school that was changing to a support centre (Jordan and Goodey, 1996). At this time it was predicted that 'all children are expected to be in mainstream schools by 1999 when the future of the last remaining special school premises will be decided'.

At the time of writing, in 2003, there are still special schools and children who are not educated within the local area. However, Newham is supporting changes of provision for children to transfer from resourced schools to their local schools. The Council's 'Pupils with Exceptional Needs: resourced and special provision' describes how this is occurring for some groups of children and schools across the borough. For example:

> The inclusion of pupils with MLD [moderate learning difficulties] and with speech and language difficulties from resourced provision is a positive outcome of inclusive practice in Newham. The setting up of the Language and Communication Service [LCSS] and the Autism Support, Development and Advice Team [ASDAT] teams also means that pupils with more complex needs can also be supported in their local schools.
>
> ... Pupils with moderate and severe learning difficulties are being placed in mainstream schools. No new placements have been made in the last 3 years of the current planning period at any resourced secondary school, and pupils have been placed successfully in mainstream secondary schools. Therefore, no proposals for any MLD provision in the secondary sector will be made in this planning period.
>
> *(Newham Council, 2002, p. 23)*

This evidence would seem to suggest that resourced schools are a 'current compromise' in which children can access both mainstream school placements and specialized support. But it is a compromise with the potential to be part of developing an inclusive educational system in the longer term, a system in which all children will have a place in their local school.

Barriers to moving on

Newham is looking to bring all pupils into local schools. There as elsewhere, however, there are children and young people who currently remain on the margins of the educational system. Is it realistic to predict that they will become fully part of the mainstream? Unit 12 considers other such marginalized groups and how they are supported.

We also need to remember that not all children will be located in their local schools while there are still grammar schools, as is the case in Dover where Aspen 2 and Archers Court are located. This kind of selective system is one of the 'structural' limits to neighbourhood inclusion that is easily forgotten. As the head of Aspen 2 said in an interview with the course team:

> Inclusive education, if it's going to be seen in its widest context can't exist in a system where one third of a school population is having its curriculum delivered in a grammar school while the remaining two thirds are having it in a secondary modern school.

The social and economic factors that act on schools and their pupils will be discussed in Units 11 and 12 when we consider social exclusion and the processes of marginalization.

A group who are more readily recognized as representing the 'limits' of inclusion are pupils with profound and multiple learning difficulties (PMLD). These are pupils who are functioning at or below the one to two year old level in most areas of development, who have additional sensory, physical or medical impairments, and who typically need a high level of support for all their activities. It is usually seen to be these within-child factors that limit inclusion. Try to keep such pupils in mind as you approach the next activity.

⭕ Activity 10.6

Cleves Primary School is resourced for pupils with PMLD. The Disability Rights Commission (DRC) interviewed the headteacher about the school's inclusive approach. The interview, reproduced below, illustrates many of the issues we have discussed in this unit and gives examples of inclusive practices within the school.

As you read the interview, consider how easily the practices that this resourced school has developed will transfer to other 'ordinary' schools. You may be able to think of a primary school in your own area. Would you see the Cleves' ethos as applicable in that school? Is this resourced school 'as far as it goes' for these pupils? Note your thoughts on these issues in your learning journal. You may wish to supplement the information in the interview by looking up SENDA and DRC information through the course website.

1   *The school has been in existence for nearly 10 years. What is the ethos of the school, and was an inclusive approach one of Cleves' main aims from the beginning?*

Cleves is part of Newham's commitment to the inclusion of pupils with special needs into mainstream primary and secondary schools. When the school opened in 1992, along with our sister school, North Beckton, we were the next stage in the development of inclusive provision in the borough. The schools were allocated a certain number of places ... for pupils with high levels of learning needs.

Staff were recruited to the school on the basis that children with severe and profound learning difficulties would be fully included in the curriculum and daily life of the school. It was never intended to have separate provision for pupils with special needs – in fact the aims were to have an experiential sensory curriculum for all children.

The first group of staff that were recruited went away for a training weekend to agree the aims and objects of an inclusive school. These are reviewed on an annual basis and provide a focus to the structure of the school.

We believe that Inclusion is not just about providing support for individual children but it is concerned with implementing a management and organisational structure that enables all children to access the curriculum whatever their learning styles or needs.

2   *How many places are available for disabled children, and what is the range of these disabilities?*

We have 32 places that are resourced for children with profound and multiple difficulties/severe learning difficulties. Included in this group are children on the autistic spectrum, children with challenging behaviour as well as children with very high learning needs. We include children who need another person to access all aspects of their life and their curriculum.

3   *How do you plan and cater for the different educational needs of these children?*

The organisation and structure of the school reflects its inclusive nature. We celebrate the open plan nature of the building with staff working in teams, planning a subject-based curriculum. The curriculum organisation is structured in a similar way to a secondary school e.g. staff planning and teaching a curriculum area for several weeks with the children moving to the room dedicated for that subject.

We use the QCA [Qualifications and Curriculum Authority] schemes of work and national strategies in literacy and numeracy.

We have developed planning sheets that require teachers to differentiate the activities as well as identifying sensory and communication activities ...

In the whole school there are organisational and management structures that promote inclusion. There is no playtime in the morning or afternoon, and built into the curriculum are opportunities for physical activities and social interaction. There is a playtime at lunchtime ...

4   *What about children who need medication? How does the school deal with this?*

The school has admitted children who have medical needs including rectal valium, catheterisation, oxygen etc. Staff in the teaching teams along with the Deputy Head/SENCo, volunteer to be trained to be able to administer medication. The training is organised and delivered by the school nursing service ...

5   *What about children with mobility and visual impairments? Is the school accessible for these particular children?*

The school is on one storey with no steps and all rooms are accessible. Staff are thoughtful about the placing of furniture to enable access to the curriculum for all children. The corridors around the school are kept as free as possible of furniture to enable free access around the building.

6   *Before a disabled pupil is admitted to the school, do you arrange a meeting(s) with parents to discuss any special arrangements that can be made?*

Most of the children with special needs start in the Early Years Wing in the nursery/reception classes. Parents/carers are encouraged to visit before their child is admitted to the school. Generally they are shown around by the Deputy Head/SENCo who spends time talking with the parents to find out about their child and to share information about the school and its organisation and structure.

The curriculum support teacher then will make a home visit to find out more about the child and their needs. The Deputy Head/SENCo and curriculum support teacher will then put together a transition programme to enable the child to settle comfortably into school ...

One of our aims is to help parents/carers to be able to trust the staff. Regular contact is kept with the parents through a daily diary and telephone conversations. After six months we call an informal review to share information on how the child is progressing and discuss any issues.

7   *What particular steps has the school taken to prevent any pupil being discriminated against because of their disability? For example, have staff been involved in any disability awareness training?*

All parents/carers of children who are admitted to the school are made aware of its inclusive nature. It is very apparent that we welcome all families and children ...

All policies and procedures take into account the diversity of children, staff and community that use the school e.g. the behaviour policy is based on developing relationships that take into account issues associated with children with challenging behaviour.

Staff use circle times as a way of boosting children's positive self-esteem and we have used 'circle of friends' activities with particular children ...

8   *How would you say children with learning difficulties or behaviour problems fit into the school's culture?*

The organisation and structure of the wings and teamwork help to enable children with behaviour difficulties and learning needs to be successful learners.

The school has delegated resources for children outside of the resource provision who have special educational needs. We use these resources and more to employ two additional teachers and a learning support assistant to work across the school. The children have IEPs [individual education plans] ... [and] management programmes including ones for behaviour that ensure that staff are consistent in their approach to children ...

9   *How do the non-disabled children react to the disabled children? Are they supportive or does bullying occur? If bullying of a disabled child occurs because of his or her disability, how does the school address this?*

The ethos of the school is based on the celebration of difference. This is reflected in every aspect, the organisation and structure, the curriculum, the learning environment etc. The ethos of the school is for children to work together and support each other.

Children work and learn in groups that include all the children in the school.

Staff make it very clear to children that bullying of any sort is unacceptable and that there are clear consequences for dealing with any name-calling or physical abuse. The behaviour policy has clear procedures for dealing with any bullying, racist or sexist incidents. Essentially the victim is comforted; the perpetrator punished and parents informed. If there is persistent bullying then the child is excluded from their class or wing and if necessary the school.

10   *Would you say that non-disabled pupils benefit from this inclusive approach, and if so, how?*

Very clearly yes. The inclusive nature of the school means that the organisation and ethos are in place to support a range of learning needs and styles. Cleves serves a multicultural community in an inner city area with a high degree of poverty.

Staff are skilled at planning for a wide range of differentiation and working in teams is an enabling and supportive management structure.

Our results at Key Stage 1 and 2 are rising every year and last year a child achieved level 6 in science (level 4 is average for Key Stage 2).

12   *It is clear that all pupils within your school are not only 'integrated' into the school, but also actively involved and welcomed – whether they are disabled or not. Do you feel that this 'essential groundwork', especially regarding disabled pupils is undermined as they progress through the educational system? If this is so, do you think introduction of the new Special Educational Needs and Disability Act (SENDA) will eliminate this problem?*

I think that attitudes are changing all the time towards children and young people with disabilities. Society has a more positive attitude towards inclusion in schools.

In Newham, children with a range of learning needs are included into secondary schools just as they are in primary and nursery provision.

I think SENDA is a very positive and supportive mechanism to enable inclusion to develop further. It provides the basis for Local Authorities to strategically plan for the inclusion of pupils with special needs. It identifies that inclusion is not just about physical access but also about access to learning and the curriculum. Linked with the new code of practice it supports parents/carers in expressing a preference for their child to go to the local school and be part of the community in which they live.

(Disability Rights Commission, 2002)

• • • • • • • • • • • • • • • • • • •

It is worth raising the point that having 32 children with PMLD in one local primary school is not what would happen if children where included in their local school. The numbers would be much smaller.

What advantages and disadvantages do you think exist with this? Does the resourced model give staff the chance to build their expertise? Would the curriculum be differentiated more or less with fewer pupils? How might the presence of large numbers of children influence the way they are perceived by their peers or the ethos of the school? You may want to include some of these points in your response to the last activity in this unit.

Activity 10.7

At the start of this unit you noted your thoughts concerning the existence of a diversity of provision. What is your position now on there being a range of educational units and resourced schools? Compare your thoughts with the notes you made for Activity 10.1. If your views have changed, what factors have most influenced this? If your views are still the same, what would need to be different in order for your views to change? You might like to try to explain your thoughts on this matter to a friend and hear their response to your position.

6 Conclusion

We have presented information about separate units within mainstream schools, additionally resourced schools and schools in transition with the aim of developing an understanding of different versions of inclusion. We have explored what, for each of us, counts as inclusive. In doing this we have suggested that this judgement is not a simple issue of inclusive or not inclusive. Inclusion can be seen as a multi-faceted and fluid process, driven by particular beliefs. We highlighted the importance of attitudes and interpersonal relationships in developing inclusion, and these are reflected in the decisions and interactions that take place in schools and classrooms on a moment-by-moment basis.

Support staff are key personnel and the way in which they are used and perceived by everyone, and particularly the pupils, is significant. They have vital roles to play in ensuring that pupils are an integral part of the school while, at the same time, addressing issues related to an individual's impairment or difficulty in learning. Collaborative approaches between professionals and children have been suggested as one way of supporting inclusion.

What may help resourced schools to move towards further inclusion is when disabled children and communities of disabled people are part of the decision making process and act as key influences on the provision. Whether within the school itself or between professional groups, the most important change is the change that occurs between people. Without this change, separate units and additionally resourced schools risk recreating the special within the mainstream. Instead of representing a continuum of provision, they may mean a range of segregation – an end point rather than a step along the way. Separate units and resourced schools have the potential to be constructed as un/satisfactory compromises, or they may be used as stepping stones towards inclusive education.

References

Association of Teachers and Lecturers (2000) 'Blind teacher made to feel a "burden" wins discrimination case'. Available from: http://www.askatl.org.uk/news/press_releases/2000/jul2000/Pn0045.htm (accessed January 2004).

British Association of Teachers of the Deaf (BATOD) (2003) 'Communication modes currently in use in the education of deaf children and young people in the UK'. Available from: http://www.batod.org.uk/communicationmodes_nf.htm (accessed February 2003).

Bowers, T. (1997) 'Supporting special needs in the mainstream classroom: children's perceptions of the adult role', *Child: care, health and development*, **23**(3), pp. 217–32.

Centre for Studies on Inclusive Education (CSIE) (1997) 'Working towards inclusion 1997', January: http://inclusion.uwe.ac.uk/csie/csie97.htm (accessed June 2002).

Centre for Studies on Inclusive Education (CSIE) (1996) 'Working towards inclusion 1996', July: http://inclusion.uwe.ac.uk/csie/csie96.htm (accessed January 2004).

Channel 4 (2002) Notes for *Count me In* series, London, Schools Interactive, Channel 4.

Chappell, A. L. (1994) 'A question of friendship: community care and the relationships of people with learning difficulties', *Disability and Society*, **9**(4), pp. 419–34.

Cuckle, P. (1997) 'The school placement of pupils with Down's syndrome in England and Wales', *British Journal of Special Education*, **24**(4), pp. 175–9.

Cuckle, P. and Wilson, J. (2002) 'Social relationship and friendship among young people with Down's syndrome in secondary school', *British Journal of Special Education*, **29**(2), pp. 66–71.

Department for Education and Skills (DfEE) (1997) *Excellence for All Children: meeting special educational needs*, London, DfEE (Green Paper).

Disability Rights Commission (2002) 'Cleves Primary School interview'. Available from: http://www.drc-gb.org/newsroom/newsdetails.asp?id=272&section=1 (accessed January 2004).

Evans, J. and Lunt, I. (2002) 'Inclusive education: are there limits?', *European Journal of Special Needs Education*, **17**(1), pp. 1–14.

Hardman, M. and Worthington, J. (2000) 'Educational psychologists' orientation to inclusion and assumptions about children's learning', *Educational Psychology in Practice*, **16**(3), pp. 349–60.

Jordan, L. and Goodey, C. (1996) *Human Rights and School Change: the Newham story*, Bristol, Centre for Studies on Inclusive Education.

Lacey, P. (2001) 'The role of learning support assistants in the inclusive learning of pupils with severe and profound learning difficulties', *Educational Review*, **53**(2), pp. 158–67.

Lance, G. D. (2002) 'Distance learning and disability: a view from the instructor's side of the virtual lectern'. Available from: http://www.rit.edu/~easi/itd/itdv08nl/lance.htm (January 2004).

Mackey, S. and McQueen, S. M. A. J. (1998) 'Exploring the association between integrated therapy and inclusive education', *British Journal of Special Education*, **25**(1), pp. 22–7.

Miller, O. (2002) 'The impact of theories of 'New Public Management' on the provision of support services for low-incidence special needs', *European Journal of Special Needs Education*, **17**(1), pp. 67–75.

McGregor, E. and Campbell, E. (2001) 'The attitudes of teachers in Scotland to the integration of children with autism into mainstream schools', *Autism*, **5**(2), pp, 189–207.

Mittler, P. (2000) *Working Towards Inclusive Education*, London, David Fulton.

Newham Council (2002) 'Pupils with exceptional needs, resourced and special provision' in *Inclusive Education Strategy 2001–2004*. Available from: www.newham.gov.uk/education/adobe/SEN/Inclupt5.pdf (accessed January 2004).

Powers, S. (2001) 'Investigating good practice in supporting deaf pupils in mainstream schools', *Educational Review*, **53**(2), pp 181–9.

Shanker, A. (1995) 'Full inclusion is neither free nor appropriate', *Educational Leadership*, **52**(4), pp. 18–21.

Somerset County Council (no date) 'Excellence for all children in Somerset: Somerset's response to the Green Paper', Taunton, Somerset County Council.

Traustadottir, R. (2000) 'Friendship: love or work?' in Traustodottir, R. and Johnson, K. (2000) (eds) *Women with Intellectual Disabilities: finding a place in the world*, London, Jessica Kingsley.

van Gurp, S. (2001) 'Self-concept of deaf secondary school students in different educational settings', *Journal of Deaf Studies and Deaf Education*, 6(1), pp. 54–69.

UNIT 11   Learning from experience

Prepared for the course team by Caroline Roaf and Kieron Sheehy

Contents

1 Introduction

This unit and the next consider the relationship between short- and long-term strategies to promote inclusion. In general, two kinds of activity are required to combat marginalization and disadvantage such as permanent exclusion from school, homelessness or abuse. A short-term 'reactive' response is needed to deal with the immediate threat, and a long-term 'preventive' response is needed to improve the system as a whole.

In practice, short-term responses tend to focus on immediate risks to life chances, or even to life itself. In extreme situations, when a young person is faced with, for example, permanent exclusion from school, homelessness, abuse or custody, the immediate response may be anger, frustration or grief: why is this happening to me, or to my pupils/clients, now? Those close to the young person often ask themselves what they might have done differently in the short term.

Once the emergency is over, negative feelings can take more positive forms. People ask themselves how, in the long term, the system as a whole might be improved to prevent such situations arising. How can the lessons learned from the day-to-day experiences of meeting the diverse needs of individual children and young people be transformed into changes to society, to the system as a whole? The metaphor of 'upstream' and 'downstream', described in Section 2 of this unit, helps us to tackle this question. The issue of how our willingness to learn from each other can help society to learn to become more inclusive forms the core of Units 11 and 12.

This unit and Unit 12 provide opportunities to explore the relationship between reactive experience and preventive measures to promote inclusion. We consider the part played by personal experience, whether of injustice or of that which is simply 'new', in generating strategies designed to promote inclusion and prevent exclusion. We also look at some of the principles and values underpinning the idea of prevention. Long-term, preventive strategies can be national or local, universal or targeted. We look at examples of all of these.

While this unit emphasizes preventive work and Unit 12 focuses on the management of immediate circumstances, both seek to illustrate the centrality of the relationship between the two.

Learning outcomes

By the end of this unit you will:

- recognize the relationship between short- and long-term measures to promote inclusion;
- have reflected on how the perspectives and language used to describe this relationship have developed over time;
- understand how this relationship is played out in schools and communities;
- be familiar with a range of current preventive strategies to promote inclusion.

Resources for this unit

In the course of your study of this unit you will be asked to read the following chapters:

- Reader 1, Chapter 22, 'Costing the future' by Sally Holtermann.
- Reader 2, Chapter 6, 'Early intervention in emotional and behavioural difficulties: the role of nurture groups' by Paul Cooper and Jane Lovey.

2   Upstream and downstream

The metaphor

Workers in aid agencies and development studies use a graphic metaphor for the key relationship between what must be done immediately in response to an urgent problem, crisis or injustice and what long-term strategies can be devised to prevent them arising. They tell a story, adapted to suit local conditions, of the women in a riverside village whose husbands have been taken away to fight, or to work elsewhere. After many weeks waiting, with no news, they begin to find bodies floating downstream. Some they save, others are already dead. Determined to prevent further tragedies, they decide to go upstream.

The richness of this metaphor lies first in the significance it gives to the relationship between reactive and preventive responses to injustice. Second, it draws attention to the importance of observation and analysis, cause and effect. Third, the metaphor emphasizes the part that relatively powerless people can, by working together, play in redressing injustice. Once the relationship between upstream and downstream activity has been observed it is difficult to ignore, since it informs every aspect of policy and practice to promote inclusion. Even if we must at times focus on *either* reaction *or* prevention, it is the relationship between the two that informs how we think and plan our responses to individuals and groups who may be in difficulty, or, indeed, to our own experiences of marginalization.

Thinking sociologically

The following letter provides an example of how closely upstream and downstream interact:

> I speak as a lone mother who spent eight years on a sink estate in south London, who watched a bunch of lively, bright and beautiful children turn into so-called 'yobs' and 'thugs'. The biggest crime is the lack of social housing, education and healthcare; the crimes committed by young people are out of frustration and boredom ...
>
> I know exactly how they feel as I have always lived on the 'margins of society', as a single parent on benefit living in a council house. I've been homeless, dealt with violence and assault and numerous other poverty related issues. In 1994 I began a degree in film and video, specialising in documentary. I felt so strongly about issues facing my community and wanted to give a voice to the 'unvoiced'. Unknown to me at the time, my daughter was being terrorised. On her 14th birthday we found she was 20 weeks pregnant. I used my student loan to move to another area and rented a property in the private sector. Others are not as 'fortunate'. I was unable to finish my degree: I had to put my children's interest first ...
>
> My point is that to raise a child alone without a community or family network is an almost impossible task. Until people realise that children are the responsibility of all of us, it's not going to get better ... it does take a village to raise a child – when are we going to listen to them?
>
> *(Anon, 2002)*

Another way of looking at the experiences described in this letter is in terms of the relationship between structural (public) issues and daily (personal) problems. In *The Sociological Imagination*, Charles Wright Mills argued that we should examine the intimate connections between these: 'Neither the life of an individual nor the history of a society can be understood without understanding both ... [but] men [sic] do not usually define the troubles they endure in terms of historical change and institutional contradiction' (1959, p. 13). The social model of disability is a good way of doing this (see Unit 3, Section 2). Wright Mills proposed that we should try to understand social reality in terms of the meanings that social structures have for individuals.

We owe much to Sally Tomlinson (1982) for whom it was a main purpose 'to introduce Wright Mills's ... "sociological imagination" into an analysis of special education and to try to relate processes in special education to the wider social structure' (p. 173). This relationship between the private experience of inequality and injustice – for example, a child bullied at a school which doesn't acknowledge the existence of bullying – and the development of appropriate preventive measures is at the heart of the work covered in this unit and the next.

As the lone mother's letter illustrates, 'thinking sociologically', that is, using the 'sociological imagination', can suggest possible solutions to an individual's experience of injustice or crisis. Indeed, the exercise of the sociological imagination lies behind many recent approaches to child welfare in which, for example, disabled people's experience can be linked to the environment in which they live (Hendy and Pascal, 2002; Beresford and Oldman, 2002).

Activity 11.1

Bring to mind, or visit, the catchment area of a local school known to you. Housing type and conditions, street lay-out, leisure facilities as well as industrial and business use will suggest much about the public issues facing that community. A prospectus or newsletter from the school itself could provide useful supplementary information. It may describe preventive measures the school has taken to address issues as they impact on the personal lives of individual members of the community. An Ofsted report would be a useful resource, or, if you live in Scotland, the Standard and Quality Report all schools are required to produce.

What are the issues for the community and how has the school responded? Note in your learning journal any relationships that you identify between the 'public' and 'personal' levels.

If you prefer, you could do an internet postcode profile search (see course website).

Balancing upstream and downstream work

We can see the relationship between upstream and downstream echoed in the role of special educational needs co-ordinators (SENCOs), and the two dimensions of their work to promote inclusion: with the whole school and with individual children (Unit 8, Section 3; Roaf, 1998). Whole-school, upstream initiatives would include, for example, curriculum and staff development in the wake of new legislation such as the Special Educational Needs and Disability Act (SENDA) 2001 to promote a more inclusive school environment.

Downstream work tends to focus on day-to-day specialist provision for individuals. That these two dimensions are now acknowledged is a further expression of the move away from within-child 'deficit' thinking towards a broader, systems view.

In the post-1994 SEN Code of Practice years of the late 1990s SENCOs found it neither easy, nor politically 'safe', to switch to a more preventive upstream approach from the downstream trappings of identification and assessment, the collation of SEN registers and the production of individual education plans. Accordingly, upstream work often suffered in schools, a situation not helped by the rise in child poverty (see Figure 11.2 in Section 3).

In Unit 8 we mentioned Davies *et al.*'s (1999) use of concept maps to identify the perceptions of SENCOs when faced with tensions such as these. One SENCO's graphic image of her role was reproduced as Figure 8.5, which is repeated here as Figure 11.1 (overleaf). Here, the tension is expressed in terms of what can and can't be achieved. It can also be read as a portrayal of what can be achieved by someone working on their own and what might be achieved with the support of others. Would the former be more likely, in your opinion, to be reactive downstream work and the latter upstream prevention? In explaining her drawing, the SENCO comments:

> I'm really pleased to have got this job, it's what I've wanted all along, but never thought I'd get it so soon. So my picture is supposed to be optimistic ... My picture shows me juggling with 7 or 8 areas of SENCO work ... I think that, at certain times, I simply won't be able to cope with all the things required. This is why I show some things falling on the floor ... As far as I'm concerned, being a SENCO is about making decisions about what can and can't be achieved in reality ... What I shall do is to see what things are most important to my school and then try to fit them into my work pattern.
>
> *(Davies et al., 1999, p. 39)*

As a preparation for the next activity you might like to consider, in terms of pro- and reactive work, which 'things' you think would have 'fallen on to the floor' and which were regarded as 'most important to my school'.

Activity 11.2

The SEN Code of Practice sets out the following main responsibilities in the role of the SENCO in England, Wales and Northern Ireland. The list below relates to primary schools, but the role of the secondary SENCO is almost identical. In Scotland there is no post of SENCO as such. In a large primary school there

Figure 11.1   A SENCO's concept map (from Davies, Garner and Lee, 1999, p. 39).

might be a senior teacher of learning support; in a secondary school there might be principal teachers of learning support, of special educational needs and of social, emotional and behavioural difficulties.

- day-to-day operation of the school's SEN policy
- co-ordinating provision for children with special educational needs
- liaising with and advising fellow teachers
- managing learning support assistants
- overseeing the records of all children with special educational needs
- liaising with parents of children with special educational needs
- contributing to the in-service training of staff
- liaising with external agencies including the LEA's support and educational psychology services, health and social services, and voluntary bodies.

(DfES, 2001, para. 5.32)

Given what you already know about the role of the SENCO (see Unit 8 and Chapter 19 in Reader 1), consider which activities are predominantly upstream and which are predominantly downstream. What tensions do you think might arise in practice in balancing the upstream and downstream aspects of this role?

How might teaching assistants and other support staff help
SENCOs to achieve a balance?

We recalled a situation where a teaching assistant was working hard
to keep a particular child 'afloat' in the mainstream classroom. This
support, social as well as academic, was the downstream element,
helping the child to develop the skills they needed to stay and learn
in the classroom. The upstream work included the development, by
the SENCO, of a strong pastoral system within the school, the
establishment of a 'breakfast club' and school links with community
organizations. (These are discussed in Section 6.) You may have
noted examples in Unit 9's video bands.

3 From compensation to prevention: changing perspectives

Unit 3 looked at social disadvantage and the social model of
disability. It showed how post Second World War concerns focused on
what could be done to alleviate the consequences of deprivation, how
the idea of compensation meant the advantaged 'we' making up for
the gap between 'us' and 'them'. Yergin and Stanislaw (1998) suggest
that, when contrasted with 'ambulance' approaches, such welfare
measures were upstream strategies.

> The Beveridge Report ... set out social programs to slay the
> 'five giants': Want, Disease, Ignorance, Squalor, and
> Idleness (i.e., unemployment) ...
>
> Implementing the recommendations of the Beveridge
> Report, the Labor government established free medical
> care under a newly constituted National Health Service,
> created new systems of pensions, promoted better
> education and housing, and sought to deliver on the
> explicit commitment to 'full employment'. All of this
> added up to what the Laborites were to call the welfare
> state – and they were very proud to do so ...
>
> [Previously] the first state insurance schemes for
> unemployment and health and old-age pensions ... [were]
> initial steps of what was at the time called the 'ambulance
> state' ...
>
> By contrast, the comprehensiveness of the Labor Program
> of 1945 transformed Britain from a would-be ambulance
> state into the first major welfare state.
>
> *(Yergin and Stanislaw, 1998)*

Compensatory measures have, however, generally come to be seen as patronizing, a form of charity, relating fundamentally to the deficit models current at the time. In an inclusive society, prevention would preclude the need for compensation.

Looking back, we can see that the post Second World War heyday of the welfare state, with its emphasis on universal provision, was nonetheless characterized by deficit models, compensatory measures, 'diagnose and treat', and relative concepts of culture and of need. In such a climate, there was little talk of rights. The idea of the integration into mainstream society of minority groups such as children with special educational needs, or Black children, involved an expectation that these groups would adapt to the norms of the 'majority' and become 'assimilated' into society.

A generation later, in the early 1980s, the concept of inclusion was still some way off and a positive attitude towards diversity within a rights model of social justice was being promoted as a new challenge. A local education authority discussion paper on education and equality explored these ideas. Written by an advisory committee for multicultural education (ACME), with an emphasis on racial equality, the perspectives described in the document have a general application:

> The fundamental debate is to do with three main values – integration, diversity and equality. Most people support all three of these values. However, different people understand them in different ways, and combine them together into different overall outlooks. Over the last two decades three main perspectives have evolved: a perspective emphasising integration and assimilation was the basis for policy in the 1950s and 1960s; a perspective emphasising diversity and pluralism became influential in the 1970s; a perspective emphasising equality and justice, and combating racism, should be the basis for policies in the 1980s.
>
> (ACME, 1982, p. 5)

Although such a perspective was not even to begin to inform government policy for a further fifteen years, it is significant that the underlying commitment to social justice remained an influential, if not always powerful, hidden force. This commitment has found expression in a range of initiatives, some of which will be discussed in this and the following unit. In these initiatives we see that reaction to some shocking event concerning an individual or group can lead to a significant long-term, preventive, upstream response.

In a widely publicized case in Cleveland, England, in the mid 1980s, for example, 121 children were diagnosed as sexually abused, removed from their homes and placed in care. It was later decided that most of the children had not been abused and 98 were returned to their parents. *The Report of the Inquiry into Child Abuse in Cleveland* (Butler-Sloss, 1988) was published not long before the Children Act 1989, which made it mandatory for courts in England and Wales to have regard to 'the ascertainable wishes and feelings of the child' (1:3a). Major reviews of legislation concerning children and families were under way in Scotland at the same time.

The Report acknowledged children's rights – 'The child is a person and not an object of concern' (Butler-Sloss, 1988, p. 245) – and Cleveland marked a turning point in public perception of services for children. It led directly to the publication of *Working Together* (DoH/DfES and Welsh Office, 1991) which proposed a standardized structure and format for new local handbooks recommending the procedures to be gone through in local authorities concerning child abuse in their areas. As a result of Cleveland, a number of long-term preventive measures were introduced. Child Protection Registers and Panels were set up and inter-agency processes to accord with good practice were outlined. The exposure of a complex, deep-seated problem had begun to yield long-term solutions and the development of upstream policy.

Implementing such policy is never, however, a simple matter. For example, at the same time as these policies were being developed in the 1990s, the research community concerned with children's rights and welfare was accumulating a mass of powerful data that demonstrated an alarming increase in child poverty since 1979. The picture revealed by Figure 11.2 has been hard for the public to believe, let alone respond to.

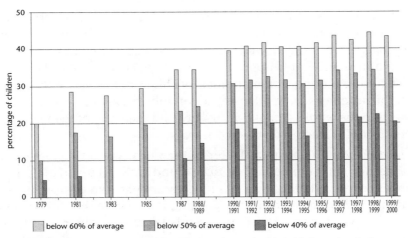

Figure 11.2   Percentage of children living in households with incomes below average after housing costs (source: Bradshaw, 2002, Figure 1)

How do you implement effective, long-term solutions in response to events such as Cleveland in the context of a general increase in child poverty? Do you use targeted or universal provision? In 1994, the

Audit Commission discussed the tension between targeted and universal provision in the following way:

> The Children Act [1989] requires authorities to identify 'children in need'. In areas such as education and primary preventive health care, the main task is to ensure worthwhile and well organized universal provision and encourage universal uptake. In others such as child protection, the task is to identify and provide services on a selective basis. In the latter case, failure to target means not only a waste of resources but also a failure to ensure the well-being of those children who slip through the net of universal services, or for whom universal provision is insufficient.
>
> *(Audit Commission, 1994, para. 10)*

Douglas Mitchell and Linda Scott describe this tension in a slightly differently way:

> ... there is a powerful tension between the *case-structured* work orientation of some agency professionals and the *program-structured* approach taken by others. Program approaches are characteristic of schools and other service agencies seeking to reach all members of a population group. Case-structured work predominates in those areas where delivery is targeted on individuals with clearly defined special needs.
>
> *(Mitchell and Scott, 1993, p. 89)*

In their view, 'case-structured education', that is, reactive work with individuals, 'remains *at the margins* of school service delivery'. Thus they suggest that the 'powerful tension' between case- and programme-structured approaches could not be resolved if schools tried to case manage large numbers of children. The very existence of a large number was, in other words, an indication of an issue affecting the whole-school community and therefore of the need for 'programme-structured', upstream work.

It is important to note that the use of the word 'tension' suggests a connection, that a balance has to be found between upstream and downstream work: the tension is a necessary one and getting the right balance is what matters. It is important, too, to note that Mitchell and Scott's conclusions are based on careful observation and analysis of data.

Those who are fully stretched managing their own difficulties or helping others tend not to have much time to influence upstream policy making. They must rely on colleagues in other parts of the system to carry out the necessary research. For example, a local policy group or independent pressure group might provide the long-term commitment needed to address the 'public' issue which has occasioned an individual's 'private' problem. Increasingly, an important function of such groups is to ensure that upstream programmes can be not only accessed, but influenced by the children and young people who need them most.

4 Generating preventive strategies

The role of experience

How can an understanding and management of *new* experiences help us to make a positive connection between reactive and preventive work? New experiences, particularly those associated with injustice, lead to work that is unpredictable, volatile and risky. However, new experiences, even the experience of a disaster, can be managed: planning and training help and almost invariably stimulate questions and research.

In *Wise Before the Event* (1993) William Yule and Anne Gold take as their starting point some major tragedies that have affected schools. They emphasize the importance of forward planning, including the development of short-, medium- and long-term action plans, in helping schools cope in the event of a tragedy. Such forward planning, which will be familiar to those working with children in any context, plays an important part in maintaining the upstream/downstream relationship.

Thus we can interpret the management of new experiences as an important means of linking programme-structured work and case-structured work. With sufficient planning, issues identified in the white water of downstream activity can be moved into the calm of upstream and, eventually, universal provision. Peter Moss and Pat Petrie consider that 'Because modernity abhors complexity and uncertainty, "crisis" is a worrying word. Crises need to be cleared up quickly. But viewed from another perspective, crisis – as questioning the taken for granted, putting a stutter into powerful narratives, creating confusion and uncertainty, making people think twice – is a hopeful word' (2002, p. 185).

The positive responses of many education services to unaccompanied under-eighteen-year-old refugees and asylum seekers, discussed in Unit 12, provide an example here. Some schools and authorities have been quick to welcome and learn from their experience of including asylum seekers and this has helped them begin to move from downstream to upstream practice. That experience and success then provide a marker for others of what can be achieved and lead directly to more inclusive practice that benefits everyone.

Inclusion, indeed, seems to be premised on a close relationship between case- and programme-structured work: what we learn from our analysis of new experiences, however harsh, feeds into our planning for whole-school improvement. A feature of classroom work is never knowing who or what will come through the door and always needing to be in a state of preparedness and able to prioritize. The example of Pen Green outlined in Unit 9 provides an excellent example of how downstream experience can transform a community.

 # Activity 11.3

This exercise is useful preparation for TMA 04.

To engage with inclusion is to engage with new challenges and experiences. Reflect on a situation that challenged your own definition of inclusion. Examples might be listening to a young person explain that she wanted to learn to write in her community language so she could write to her grandmother, or reading about a young person wanting to learn three foreign languages even though this involved a lot of writing and that was difficult for him. Or you may have come across an example in the course materials and resources.

1   Briefly describe the situation.
2   Note what was, or could have been, done to incorporate this experience into improved policy and practice.

Prerequisites of prevention

Principles and values

The articulation of the principles and values underpinning social justice and equality is a significant preventive measure because it sets out an ethos and context of expectations within which further decisions are taken. In relation to children, these key values are embodied in the 1989 United Nations Convention on the Rights of the Child (UNCRC) (UNICEF UK, 1995). Article 12 of the UNCRC (introduced in Unit 3) asserts the right of children and young people to say what they think and be listened to by adults when adults make decisions that affect them. In this unit we are concerned with such documents as a point of reference when considering proactive measures to promote inclusion.

A number of other international documents are important. The European Convention on Human Rights and the judgements of the European Court of Human Rights have had a significant influence on policy making to protect children's rights in the UK. Young people themselves have pursued their complaints in the European Court in some well-publicized cases. For example, they have challenged UK attitudes towards corporal punishment: what is to count as 'reasonable chastisement', or, in the case of juvenile defendants convicted of murder, what is to count as a fair trial?

Children in anti-smacking protest

Saturday, 15 April, 2000

Hundreds of children have marched through central London to demand an end to smacking. They paraded along the streets of Westminster chanting 'Stop the smacking', and waving placards which read 'Violence is not the answer' and 'We have rights too'. The children ended their protest at Downing Street, where they handed in a letter addressed to Tony Blair, urging him to ban all physical punishment of children. The demonstration was organised by children and teenagers from campaign group Article 12, a young people's organisation dedicated to promoting children's rights to expression.

'We want to show the government actively that we are opposed to physical punishment of children,' said one of the organisers, 16-year-old David Henry, from Manchester.

'We want to make a political statement to the whole world that children should not be smacked or hurt in any way by anyone.'

'A lot of the little children who are here today have got a lot to say but they are the ones that don't get listened to.'

Another teenage protester, Kate Wood from north London, said: 'We believe that all forms of physical punishment are wrong and therefore smacking should be illegal.'

And she criticised government proposals to tighten the law on assaults on children, which stop short of an outright ban.

'The government did a consultation document that was in very complicated language that children could not understand and they did not even bother talking to children about it,' said Kate, 14.

(BBC, 2000)

You might like to ask yourself at this point whether you think it will eventually be made illegal in the UK to physically punish a child under the age of three. There has been strong opposition to this from some, while others would go further and ban physical punishment altogether. It is interesting to recall that in the 1960s the idea of banning corporal punishment in schools was considered revolutionary.

The meetings of the World Conference on Education for All held at Jomtien in 1990 and Dakar in 2000 played a very significant part in educating world opinion on the failure to honour Article 28 of the UNCRC (the right to education). They also served to remind residents of the UK of their responsibilities towards the 12,000 or so children and young people regularly excluded from school each year during the 1990s.

Between these two meetings, the Spanish government hosted the World Conference on Special Needs Education in Salamanca in 1994, famous for the Salamanca Statement on inclusive education (UNESCO, 1994). In the light of this unit's concern with learning from experience, the conference report makes interesting reading. It shows how the links made between experience gained in different places have been followed through into general lessons that can be applied to special education universally. Inclusive education was seen to be a concept rooted in experience, even though the process by which that experience could be shared was likely to be slow, needing long-term international commitment and resources.

In May 2002, for the first time at a UN conference, 300 children were invited to attend a children's forum, held over the three days before the main meeting. There, the delegates under the age of eighteen discussed their proposals for a better world for children and then presented these to the main conference. However, as Rachel Harvey of the Children's Legal Centre reports:

Unfortunately, children's voices and demands were lost among the bickering of States, who attempted to protect their national interests at the expense of the best interests of the child. Child participants voiced disappointment with the process and the Outcome Document, which they felt did not reflect the message from the Children's Forum. An under-18 delegate from the UK said, *'We spoke, but it feels like no-one listened'*.

(Harvey, 2002, p. 3)

The participation of children in decision and policy making is likely to make policy more inclusive, so listening to their aspirations would seem to be a crucial preventive measure to promote inclusion. Getting those in power to listen is, however, notoriously difficult, hence the importance of long-term campaigns to shift public opinion.

New discourses

A by-product of the shift in perspective from deficit models to social models has been to make it possible to view children as being 'at promise' rather than 'at risk'. Beth Blue Swadener and Sally Lubeck (1995) introduced a welcome antidote to the tendency among practitioners and policy makers, reinforced by years of application of the medical model, to look for problems and difficulties in the assessment of 'need' rather than strengths and possibilities for future development.

Nonetheless, the Organisation for Economic Co-operation and Development (OECD), for example, had difficulty in finding an alternative term to 'at risk'. They found that in spite of their reservations there was general agreement about what was meant by children 'at risk', at least for the purpose of their research. These were young people who were: 'failing in school and unsuccessful in making the transition to work and adult life and as a consequence are unlikely to be able to make a full contribution to active society' (OECD, 1995, p. 21). The OECD rationalized their use of the term 'at risk' by making it clear that for them it implied an emphasis on the future and prevention; it was a means of helping them identify appropriate upstream strategies that could be recommended to the governments of all the member nations.

Peter Moss and Pat Petrie (1997) take us further, however. They call for a new discourse based on a concept of the child as 'a citizen, equal in value to an adult, with a voice to be listened to and with accompanying rights ... an active member of a *community* and *society* as well as a family ...' (p. 11). This concept asserts a principle which helps us to break free of the notion that children can be categorized simplistically as either 'at risk' or 'not at risk'. The emphasis on principle enables us to reach forward to a more inclusive world in which we can live together and learn from each other. In such a world, it would be within our power to set up systems in which upstream strategies develop in response to downstream experience. As the 'voices' heard in this course attest, it is only through listening to, and learning from, each other's experience that such systems can be developed.

It is significant, therefore, that over thirty years after the 1970 Education (Handicapped Children) Act, the initiative and voice of disabled people are once again moving the inclusion debate forward for everyone. If the 1981 Education Act shifted mind sets from segregation to integration, the 1995 Disability Discrimination Act and the 2001 SENDA between them have the potential to move us forward to more physically inclusive communities in which the views of children are sought and responded to. This ground is covered extensively in Unit 3, but is worth reiterating here in relation to proactive measures to promote inclusion. Access encourages visibility and voice. Both are required in order to create inclusive communities in which the physical sight and sound of diversity tell its own story.

Putting children first

Two reports from the Audit Commission (1992a; 1992b) exposed very large sums of money unaccounted for in early 1990s special educational needs provision (£1.5 billion in 1991/92). Their emphasis on the need for close monitoring and evaluation of initiatives and legislation which impact on children has come to be seen as an essential safeguard of children's rights and well-being. In a research project commissioned by Barnardos, Sally Holtermann was asked to 'consider the policies of all the main spending departments, not just those that would have an obvious direct effect on children such as education, but also those that would have an indirect effect' (Holtermann, 1996, p. 3). She concluded that Britain was under-investing in its children. More could and should be done, but 'there must be a greater willingness to spend more on public services for children than in recent years, and to give higher priority to promoting a social and economic environment in which all children can reach more of their potential' (p. 12).

◯ Activity 11.4

• • • • • • • • • • • • • • • • • • • •

Now read Reader 1, Chapter 22, 'Costing the future' by Sally Holtermann.

1   As you read, use your own experience of children and young people to reflect on the events or experiences which made you aware of the need for some of the upstream proposals suggested by Holtermann.

2   In making her list of 'programmes and policies for significant benefits for children and young people', Holtermann suggests

that 'there is room for lengthy debate about which things should be included and which left out ... ' (p. 268). In your learning journal, make a note of the programmes and policies you would like to see prioritized.

Personal experience clearly affected what we considered to be priorities. We saw childcare and good quality day care as major upstream issues in need of prioritization.

A measure of the degree to which policy makers are prepared to put children first is expressed in the idea of 'child impact analysis'. This, according to Lisa Payne, principal policy officer at the National Children's Bureau, is 'a rather ornate way to describe a simple concept' (2002, p. 132):

> Proposals for policy, legislation, service restructuring, planning, or monitoring should be analysed for their potential impact on children and young people. It is a way of ensuring that we take into account how a proposed new motorway, an immigration service detention centre, a closed public park, a benefits office or a 24-hour pub might affect the children who live near it or who will use it. It demands that we look at their needs as well as the needs of the motorist, the Immigration and Nationality Department, the local authority, benefits staff and their customers, and the local drinkers and football fans.

> For example, it may help those designing or protesting against a new motorway to assess the effect it could have on child accident rates in an already dangerously built-up area. It could convince benefits staff to install a small play area for young children to keep them occupied while their parents wait to be interviewed. The process renders children more visible because it requires us to remember that they too count. It improves services because they become more responsive to the needs of those who use them. Child impact analysis is a process, an evaluative tool – not a definitive result.

> Child impact analysis should begin with a series of questions.

> - Will this have any direct implications for children or children's issues?

> - Will this have any indirect significant effect on children?

- What impact will this have on the general welfare of children?

- Will this adversely affect other policy areas, agencies or others in their work with children?

- What do children and young people think about this proposal?

- Is this the best way of responding to their needs?

(Payne, 2002, p. 130)

This questioning process is a familiar evaluative tool, and, as with any other evaluation, child impact analysis is intended to be used at all stages of the policy-making and legislative process. Unusually, however, child impact analysis privileges children. This is particularly significant because there has been an almost total refusal to respect children as fellow citizens or treat them with dignity, let alone invite them to contribute to policy making. Lisa Payne comments that even in areas such as education, 'where children should be at the core of any changes made, they would be obliged to "fit" into the system' (Payne, 2002, p. 130). If inclusive education is about making education more responsive to children – fitting with them – then children must be put first.

Recognizing children and young people as citizens

Although the revised Code of Practice (DfES, 2001) refers more strongly than previously to the participation of young people, particularly in the preparation of their individual education plans (IEPs), it stops short of suggesting they might also have a voice in the policy making of the school in which those plans are to be implemented. This contrasts, as the following quotation suggests, with the views of the Government's Children and Young People's Unit (CYPU).

We want all of our children and young people to be assured of ...

- chances to contribute to their local communities – feeling heard and being valued as responsible citizens – shaping their lives and their futures.

(CYPU, 2001a, para. 3.2)

While there has been some acceptance that children have a right to be listened to when the downstream initiatives affecting them individually (their personal concerns) are being discussed, very little notice has been taken of their opinions when their thoughts turn to upstream thinking and innovation. Yet, when children are given an opportunity to express a view and make suggestions, whether at the United Nations or for a newspaper, they often do so with originality, sensitivity and humanity. Take the example of 'The School I'd Like' competition. When asked to put forward their suggestions, children produced what should be a blueprint for all school design. The *Education Guardian* summarized their ideas in a 'Children's Manifesto':

> The School We'd Like is:
>
> > A beautiful school
> >
> > A comfortable school
> >
> > A safe school
> >
> > A listening school
> >
> > A flexible school
> >
> > A respectful school
> >
> > A school without walls
> >
> > A school for everybody
>
> *(Birkett cited in Burke and Grosvenor, 2003)*

We are led to wonder what child impact analysis would have made of the testing and targets influence in education.

Activity 11.5

Use the course website to access UNICEF and The Message from the Children's Forum, delivered to the UN Special Session in May 2002.

The young people quoted there illustrate the same ability as the entrants to 'The School I'd Like' competition to prioritize, and the same pithy attention to essentials and to upstream thinking. You might like to browse through this website for evidence of the continued involvement of children in UN debates.

As an alternative, you could ask some pupils to give you examples of the ways in which they are consulted about how their school is organized and what it offers them. If their school has a council, you could ask them how this functions and what matters are discussed there. In Scotland, for example, pupil councils have been set up in many schools, both primary and secondary, and since 2003 they have to be consulted, along with other bodies such as the parent–teacher association, the school board, etc., on the school's development plan.

It is gratifying to find the *Schools for the Future: Building Bulletin* (DfES, 2002) adopting at least some aspects of the Children's Manifesto in its recommendations, and to find some schools in which pupils have played a significant part in building and planning decisions. And the children's views of their new schools?

> The library is beautiful – the spiral staircase and the windows make it a peaceful place to work.
>
> The organisation is really great. All exits are easy to get to. You can get from one place to another with the minimum of fuss.
>
> I am proud of the school.
>
> *(DfES, 2002, p. 2)*

Children's councils, whether in school or as part of local government, or internationally as part of a UN conference, have had to wait a long time to reach the point at which they can influence policy in areas such as school design. Schools rarely consult children formally on matters such as the appointment of a new headteacher, the curriculum, sanctions or any of the many decisions which impact on their experience of school (Payne, 2002). Gary Thomas and Andrew Loxley (2001) include 'ensuring the minutes of the School Council are routinely taken on the governing body agenda' (p. 60) in a list of indicators of a move away from deficit-laden practice towards an emphasis on the creation of a humane environment. The implication is that this desirable state of affairs is some way off. This does indeed appear to be the case: A. S. Neill's Summerhill (Neill, 1926), where children did have a say in the running of the school, is regularly held up as a dreadful warning rather than a shining example by those fearful of sharing power with under-eighteens.

Nonetheless, attitudes have been changing rapidly in recent years. For example, the Oxfordshire Children's Rights Checklist, which children were invited to help devise, devotes five of its nineteen points to 'seeking views':

> 13. The organisation is committed to asking and involving children and young people as suggested by county guidelines.
>
> 14. There are systems to ensure children and young people's views are asked for, listened to, and acted upon in an ongoing way.
>
> 15. Views are actively asked for from groups of children and young people whose views are less likely to be heard.
>
> 16. Changes have been made as a result of asking young people.
>
> 17. There are child-friendly ways to make complaints which children and young people actually use.
>
> *(Maclagan, 2002, p. 135)*

Since 2001 Lawrence Sheriff School in Warwickshire has involved members of the school council in the interviewing of staff. Four interviewers are elected by the council as a whole, and each asks the candidate two questions, such as 'Why would I enjoy being in your lessons?' There is also an opportunity for the candidate to ask the pupils questions. The experience is seen as positive and has encouraged pupil participation in a range of school issues (DfES, 2003).

Pupils have their say in a school council.

Developments in learning theory and psychology have played their own part in promoting children's rights through the attention now given to listening to children as a crucial part of the teaching and learning process. Paying close attention to how children learn and what teachers think (Hart, 2000) has become an accepted part of good teaching. When adults listen with attention, trust develops and confidence in children's ability to participate responsibly as fellow citizens grows (Collins *et al.*, 2002). It is on these foundations that peer mentoring and counselling and other initiatives such as training primary school pupils to be mediators have developed.

Peer mediation involves pupils being trained to offer a conflict resolution service at break and lunchtime for peers who have fallen out with each other (Cremin, 2002, p. 138). Initiatives of this kind are developing in many schools. Some focus on social inclusion in the most immediate way: Funky Friends and Bench Buddies, some as young as five and six, take turns to sit on a particular bench in the playground and anyone feeling sad, lonely or left out can come and sit beside them. If this isn't inclusion and citizenship, what is?

Children's voices express needs that adults share. They can express these needs with an arresting freshness and originality. If children are our hope for the future, their voices should be listened to and their needs met, if only as a matter of self-interest.

5 Prevention: national strategies

Early intervention

Early intervention must be one of the most appealing, the most obviously beneficial, uncontroversial and wholly preventive of strategies. It is surely, one might think, uniquely upstream. Who could not wish to give every child the best possible start in life? The lone mother whose letter we quoted at the beginning of Section 2 would have given much for some early intervention. Yet early intervention is not so straightforward. It in fact gives us one of our most useful insights into the complexity of the relationship between reactive and proactive measures.

Early intervention can be discriminatory and humiliating and it can evoke prejudice. It can be directed at people who find it invasive while missing others who might want it. Nor is it invariably upstream in the sense of identifying and tackling root causes. For example, the early detection and treatment of emotional and behavioural difficulties in children tends to be dissociated from the stressful effects of factors such as poverty on children in general. Furthermore, while early intervention would be plainly beneficial (in our letter-writer's example, to support the baby), it must be balanced by, or at least not pursued to the exclusion of, 'late' intervention (that is, support for the mother).

Or take the example of a cash-strapped headteacher called to a meeting of colleagues in neighbouring schools to consider the problem of teenage persistent truants. Will existing resources be spent on early intervention with younger children and will the older truants be abandoned? And if it becomes easy to abandon one, then why not more? After all, it might be argued, what good will it do to chase after them? Yet the example which could be provided of adolescents being supported successfully into adult life would in itself be an effective preventive measure for younger children, affirming young people's resilience and optimism and giving confidence to the families, carers and teachers of young children.

The context in which early intervention strategies are promoted has to be examined very critically. To what extent are these strategies targeted or universal? Targeted provision has a place, but societies moving towards inclusion will want to be sure that the lessons learned inform universal provision. In this spirit, Peter Moss and Pat Petrie question the purpose of much previous and current intervention with children, especially young children. They argue for:

a rethinking of public provisions for children ... [one which] understands provisions as environments of many possibilities – cultural and social, but also economic, political, ethical, aesthetic, physical – some predetermined, others not, some initiated by adults, others by children: it presumes unknown resources, possibilities and potentials. These environments are understood as more public places for children to live their childhoods, alongside the more private domain of the home.

(Moss and Petrie, 2002, p. 9)

In this unit we are trying to look holistically at the provision needed to educate a child. Only as part of a whole system can we create the structures needed to resolve difficult issues, and the success of the system as a whole will be judged by how effective the arrangements are to prevent difficulties arising in the first place. Such a system will need to be capable of effectively co-ordinating upstream and downstream activities. Strategies that promote early intervention give us some classic examples of how the relationship between downstream and upstream develops in practice and why a close relationship between the two is so important to the progress of inclusion. The next reading provides an example of such a strategy.

◯ Activity 11.6

. . . .

Now read Reader 2, Chapter 6, 'Early intervention in emotional and behavioural difficulties: the role of nurture groups' by Paul Cooper and Jane Lovey.

As you read, make notes in your learning journal tracing the progress from downstream experience to upstream policy making. Note especially factors such as the passage of time, the numbers of children involved, the cost of policy implementation and the value attributed to this initiative as a vehicle to promote inclusion.

This reading also provides an opportunity to reflect on the role of close observation and detailed research in the development of upstream strategies. Although this article is written by academics, practitioners were closely involved in the research process. How, in a future study, would you like to see young people themselves involved in this research?

. . . .

Universal provision; targeted provision

Universal provision is designed to improve and/or maintain adequate living standards for all. These are the kinds of activities which feature in the follow-up reports required by, for example, the ten-yearly World Summits for Children. As one of the richest countries in the world, the UK is expected to meet targets to aid other countries, but it must also put its own house in order. Child and family health standards as well as general improvements in standards of education, health and safety, housing and the environment are examples. Similarly, the UK is expected to demonstrate its commitment to honouring the UNCRC in relation to some of the Articles in the Convention considered in Section 4. The setting up of the Children and Young People's Unit is one response to this.

It is, however, going to be hard work to achieve the Government's aim to abolish child poverty by 2020. According to the Government Statistical Office, there were still 4.1 million children living in poverty in 2000 (End Child Poverty, 2002; see also Figure 11.2). Moreover, these overall figures include groups of children, such as those from Bangladeshi and Pakistani families, who are disproportionately affected by family poverty. The national pattern is for children as a whole to be disproportionately represented in low-income households (Rahman *et al.*, 2001), making disabled children with special educational needs in those households even more vulnerable. It is disappointing to find, therefore, that the force of international opinion still seems to be needed to secure a better deal for children in the UK. Reporting on its implementation of the goals of the 1990 World Summit for Children, the Government states that:

> In the UK, we have already met and surpassed many of the World Summit's targets, for health, sanitation and education. But we are not complacent. As this Report shows, our children are vulnerable to different threats, from crime, drugs and the manifold consequences of poverty and social exclusion. The Government is tackling those. We have set up a Cabinet Committee to co-ordinate policies affecting children and young people at risk, appointed a minister for Young People and established a Children and Young People's Unit. The Unit has responsibility for developing an overarching strategy for all children and young people in England and of organising consultation events with young people to make sure their voices are heard in central government.
>
> *(Foreign and Commonwealth Office, 2001)*

The Children's Strategy, a product of the Children and Young People's Unit (CYPU) and one of the most encouraging documents to come out of government in connection with the implementation of Article 12 of the UNCRC, is universal in intent and participatory in approach. Its purpose is to develop an overarching strategy covering all services for children and young people. The foreword to the document declares that:

> Every child and young person deserves the best possible start in life, to be brought up in a safe, happy and secure environment, to be consulted, listened to and heard, to be supported as they develop into adulthood and maturity and to be given every opportunity to achieve their full potential. The government proposals for a new strategy for all children and young people are about making sure that this becomes a reality for all.
>
> *(CYPU, 2001b)*

The universal provision we take for granted today – for example, easy access to clean drinking water, elementary education and primary health care – had to be campaigned for over many years. And existing universal provision still needs to be defended. You may recall the debate engendered by a case in May 2002 when a parent served a prison sentence for failing to ensure her child's attendance at school. It was suggested at the time that parents of persistent truants should lose their child benefit – a universal provision which should not, as a matter of principle, be withheld as a punishment. Substantial increases in child benefit are thought to be one of the most effective means of lifting children out of poverty (BBC, 2002).

Within education and the other primary care agencies we can recognize cases of universal provision that act, or are intended to act, as preventive measures for all children and families. In England and Wales the national curriculum and its attendant strategies for literacy and numeracy would be examples, although these are marred by other aspects of education policy such as testing, which means that as strategies they cause further problems.

The 'healthy schools' concept was introduced in the 1997 White Paper *Excellence in Schools* (DfEE, 1997, p. 63) and followed through a year later in the Green Paper *Our Healthier Nation* (DoH/DfES, 1998). The Healthy Schools Programme sets out to 'improve standards of health and education and to tackle health inequalities. Its aim is to make children, teachers, parents and communities more aware of the opportunities that exist in schools for improving health' (Wired for Health, 2002). The programme's major components included safer travel, healthy eating, and pupil and teacher health. The National Healthy School Standard also proposed in the Green Paper was based on the idea that a healthy school was a key factor in improving children's health and education. In making recommendations for a possible model, local health and education professionals were brought together to develop an understanding of what the nature and purpose of a 'healthy school' might be.

Healthy schools

Time for fruit in a Scottish primary school.

In Scotland children in the first two years of primary school are to be given free fruit in a bid to improve eating habits. The move is part of Scottish Executive plans to invest £63m to raise the nutritional standard of school meals and increase the size of portions.

(BBC, 2003)

An improved diet helps children get the most out of their education and can improve health in both the short and long term. Child Poverty Action Group (CPAG) believes that the development of a strategy to promote healthy eating would be an investment in the health and education of Scottish school children.

(Child Poverty Action Group, 1999)

'Quality Protects' is a preventive strategy still closely linked to targeted support to allow disadvantaged children and young people to take advantage of universal services such as education and health (DoH, 1998). Subtitled 'transforming services for children', the programme was initiated in 1998 as part of New Labour's commitment to improving the lives of disadvantaged and vulnerable children: looked after children (cared for by social services), those involved with the Child Protection Service and others, including disabled children, defined as in need. In England, regional development workers in four large social care regions work alongside smaller regional offices to help councils implement the Quality Protects programme.

Activity 11.7

At this point you might like to use the course website to access the Quality Protects site and get a flavour of the range of work covered in the different regions. What would you say best characterizes their activities? We suggest you make a note of the ways in which regional development workers assist local groups to achieve the programme's objectives.

Alternatively, you might reflect on your experience as a child of factors such as housing, health care, education and opportunities for leisure and outdoor recreation. What were the positive and negative effects on your life?

Our reflections on our childhood experience generated a lot of ideas and emotions about the positive impact of upstream social measures. Some of these were so embedded in our early lives that we only became aware of the effects as a result of this exercise. For example:

As a member of an immigrant family, I think that good quality council housing made a big impact on my early life. We moved from a council flat to a council house with a nice little garden and an allotment just over the fence. It really helped us have a sound basic quality of life.

It was a good start. There was a mobile library and a local health centre that included a dentists, which was completely free. And we got free milk at primary school. There was a community swimming pool which we used a lot in the summer. Public sports facilities were quite rare, so we would often get into trouble for playing on the estate when we got older.

Later I went to a local comprehensive school and was given a grant to go to university. I feel that I was fortunate. It's much harder for children from my background today.

The 'small print' in documents relating to Quality Protects initiatives records a strong focus on research, evaluation, inter-agency work and the participation of practitioners, parents and children. Taken as a whole, the strategies used to promote participation appear to have been successful because they have encouraged 'news from the riverbank' to filter back up to the decision and policy makers.

The initiatives discussed in the rest of this section are national in that they emanate from, and are partly funded by, central government, but they generally depend on various forms of partnership with, and financial support from, local businesses and charities. Some of this provision is targeted at areas of the highest social disadvantage, but it is nonetheless clearly and deliberately preventive. Such programmes are closely influenced by downstream experience, but do not allow this to distract them from pursuing the upstream initiatives that experience leads them to. They tend to be inter-agency and responsive to local circumstances, and they can be innovative. They are the kind of strategies one might expect inclusive communities to develop.

We mention Connexions and the Children's Fund here, but others such as Health Action Zones, Education Action Zones, Youth Offending Teams, the Excellence in Cities programme and Regional Co-ordination Partnerships may operate in your area.

Connexions, which began in 2002, is a multi-disciplinary government service for all thirteen to nineteen year olds in England. There is a set of key principles, and core services are expected, but it is based on local partnerships with scope for local development and innovation. 'Young people can expect access to a service that will cater for their needs, whether straightforward or complex, as and when they require it' (Connexions, 2001, p. 2).

While the provision is universal in England, the impetus came from the experience of socially excluded young people. In an interesting critique of Connexions, Lisa Payne describes how the concept arose from Social Exclusion Unit researchers' concern at 'the 9% of the age group who fall outside the education system ... They proposed a new youth support service – Connexions – which would be universal but offer priority to those between the ages of 13 and 19 who are most at risk of disaffection and disengagement' (Payne, 2002, p. 130).

Set up and funded by the Children and Young People's Unit 'to provide support for 5–13 year olds who are showing signs of difficulty', the Children's Fund is intended to fill the gap between Sure Start, the programme for under-fives, and Connexions. While Connexions is multi-agency in some respects but based within the education service, the Children's Fund is clearly located between agencies. Local Children's Fund partnership boards place a high priority on achieving a balance of membership, representing statutory and voluntary organizations and community, parent and faith groups. Including the views of children and young people at board level is also a high priority. The Children's Fund is expected 'to support child mentoring and counselling initiatives and help the voluntary sector provide local solutions to the problems of child poverty' (Foreign and Commonwealth Office, 2001).

The strategies discussed in this section, initiated by central government, combine universal and targeted provision with the aim of preventing social exclusion. There are other essentially downstream initiatives directed at specific issues, for example, youth offending, child and adolescent mental health, the care of children at risk of abuse or homelessness, teenage pregnancy, or children caring for family members. Looking at these initiatives together, we can see the development of some interesting trends: inter-agency partnerships; combinations of universal and targeted provision; emphasis on long-term solutions; 'tight' central control of principles, core services and funding, with 'loose' responses to local circumstances; research and evidence-based practice, benchmarks, outcomes and targets.

6 Prevention: local strategies

In this section we look at initiatives that may seek financial support from local and national charities and government, but tend to rely on the work of individuals and local groups. They respond to local needs as and when they are perceived, often drawing on good (funded) practice observed elsewhere.

There are many generally advantaged areas with relatively small pockets of socially disadvantaged families and children, perhaps two or three families in a village or street whose plight is extreme. Or there may be poor, or very expensive, housing, inadequate transport and distance from mainstream city services to contend with. These areas tend to be outside the remit of the major national strategies. We discuss here a very few examples from the extensive range of initiatives that address such issues. Some have attracted national interest and acclaim, while others have been influential simply through the positive experiences of inclusion in action they have offered local communities. These initiatives illustrate vividly how close the relationship is between experience and response, the relationship captured in the upstream/downstream metaphor. Behind every national initiative or current household name in social policy, whether it is Sure Start, breakfast clubs or one-stop shops, stand a host of unpaid voluntary-sector activists who saw that initiative was needed and took it.

Breakfast clubs and after-school activities

Breakfast clubs and similar initiatives are rooted in child-centred, community-based concepts of schooling that see education and care as part of a whole rather than as separate entities. The ways in which schools have responded to the tension between education and care have changed as social conditions and social attitudes have changed. Employment patterns, especially for parents and carers, changes in the cost of living and changes in eating habits and knowledge of nutrition are particularly relevant. Over the last fifty years the UK has seen a number of approaches to the issue of free milk/meals for some/ all.

The idea of offering children a breakfast at school is both simple and highly innovative, particularly in the UK. Whereas the UK tends to maintain a strict separation between education and care, US experience going back to the 1960s suggests that such programmes can enhance academic performance and reduce behaviour problems. Nurture groups, which incorporate giving and sharing food, can help to develop trusting and satisfactory relationships between adults and children (Bennathan and Boxall, 2000).

Catherine Watson and Christine Marr describe the rationale for their school's breakfast club initiative:

> [Carden] is a special school for primary aged children with emotional and behavioural difficulties (EBD). The school operates a shared placement system with all pupils attending mainstream school for a part of their week. The time spent at mainstream school is gradually built up until the pupil is attending full time. This usually happens over a one- or two-year period ...
>
> The Breakfast Club was started because it was realised that many of the students were not eating breakfast before being picked up by the school bus. A factor in this may be that many of our pupils come from areas of high social deprivation as evidenced by the fact that seventy per cent receive free school meals. In addition, around half of our students are on medication for attention deficit/ hyperactivity disorder (AD/HD) ... skipping breakfast can lead to poor nutrition ...
>
> In addition to the health benefits to children of introducing the Breakfast Club, we also hoped to see a positive effect on school ethos and gains in student behaviour and social skills.

(Watson and Marr, 2003, p. 15)

Predictably, the scheme was very successful, not least as part of the preparation for life in a mainstream school. Parents approved. The children enjoyed it and were involved in the planning. Staff welcomed it, some seeing it as a chance to meet their pupils in an informal setting, and pupil relationships improved. Set against the vision and principles of the CYPU's Children's Strategy (see Section 5), such initiatives, however small-scale, will surely be of interest to the Children's Fund.

At the other end of the day, large sums have been available from the New Opportunities Fund and other sources for after-school activities. An extensive range of activity is covered: tuition, maybe in an additional language or community language, creative arts and leisure and outdoor pursuits and homework clubs. Before- and after-school provision would appear to bear all the marks of an initially downstream action whose time to go upstream has come.

Emotional well-being

Modern concern to promote the emotional well-being of children is rooted in humanistic psychology dating from the 1950s. Humanistic psychology emphasizes the uniqueness of each human being. It offers an optimistic view of people, affirming their ability to make choices and develop values based on their experiences, resulting in 'personal growth'. While humanism is often associated with individual counselling, the Association for Humanistic Psychology explains clearly the implications of this approach for upstream practices.

> The difficulty of encouraging personal growth is matched by the difficulty of developing appropriate institutional and organizational environments in which human beings can flourish. Clearly, societies both help and hinder human growth. Because nourishing environments can make an important contribution to the development of healthy personalities, human needs should be given priority when fashioning social policies. This becomes increasingly critical in a rapidly changing world threatened by such dangers as nuclear war, overpopulation and the breakdown of traditional social structures.
>
> Many humanistic psychologists stress the importance of social change, the challenge of modifying old institutions and inventing new ones able to sustain both human development and organizational efficacy. Thus the humanistic emphasis on individual freedom should be matched by a recognition of our interdependence and our responsibilities to one another, to society and culture, and to the future.
>
> *(Association for Humanistic Psychology, 2002)*

This tradition in psychology is especially important for comprehensive schools which have to take a very diverse range of cultures, ethnic groups and religious creeds into account.

School counsellors

Nick Luxmoore (2000) describes the kind of work school counsellors do. Schools fortunate enough to employ or have access to counsellors rely on them heavily as people with the time and skills to listen. Youth work, inter-agency work, team building, outdoor education, anger management, conflict resolution, and the training of pupil counsellors and peer mentors are among the possible activities of school counsellors. A degree of flexibility in the way they work and a degree of detachment from colleagues in mainstream services is important to them. This combination of flexibility and detachment allows them to play an important strategic role in eliciting the key issues from their own and other people's downstream experiences.

Quiet places

Schools have been notable for their lack of physical and emotional space – a matter of such concern that whole movements have been built on the desire to provide more humane educational environments (Meighan, 1992; Steiner et al., 1995). After a generation of neglect, school building has once again become a matter of interest and innovation. Attention is being paid to colour, sound, use of quiet outdoor play spaces, perhaps a sensory garden, and the use of trees and covered outdoor 'rooms'. One Merseyside initiative, 'A Quiet Place', has been particularly effective as an early intervention strategy for children with emotional and behavioural difficulties in mainstream schools:

> In every case the room has been provided by the school, and the support of the staff and headteacher has been invaluable. Prior to the initiation of the room, training has been provided to raise staff awareness of the objectives and the techniques. The room itself has been designed to promote a sense of *peace* and *relaxation*. It contains a range of soft furnishings, bean bags and 'mini environments' including tent-like areas, cosy corners, water cascades, soft toys, plants and musical instruments. Each room has its own 'theme'. The stairwell in one school, for example, has a fairly-tale mural focused on story telling.
>
> *(Spalding, 2000, p. 129)*

Quiet Place provision, serviced by a number of therapists, was designed to benefit 'high-risk' families with children presenting 'a lack of control and pre-criminal tendencies' (Spalding, 2000, p. 129). It shares much in common with 'nurture groups', and aims for an 'increase in parental empowerment and confidence in handling children within their own family, as well as within the school and the general community' (Spalding, 2000, p. 129). Evaluation of the first cohort of children to complete the Quiet Place programme has been very positive. Some schools outside the project area have since adopted the concept and are incorporating 'quiet rooms' in their building plans.

☼ Activity 11.8

At this point we invite you to consider the role of 'quiet places' in your own life as a student. Quiet places can be physical, or they can be times set aside for reflection and personal space, perhaps on a train, car or bus journey. Identifying your need and meeting it can reduce stress and/or lead to creative thinking.

Perhaps you could create a quiet place and try it out for a week, or you could improve your existing one. Share your thoughts with another person. Do they have a quiet place? How does it help? In the context of school, what part might the existence of a quiet place play in the inclusion of children at risk of marginalization or exclusion?

Values education

At Stonesfield Primary School in Oxfordshire teachers 'give regular thought as to how values can be used to support the child as a reflective learner and promote quality teaching and learning ... As a school community we believe that the ethos of the school should be built on a foundation of values' (Hawkes, 2001). From a list of values such as trust, honesty, respect, courage, etc., one is selected every month or so to be addressed through lessons and assemblies so that it permeates the curriculum. The 'values' component of assemblies also offers a *shared period* of emotional space and calm in the school day. These values are used as 'the basis for the social, intellectual, emotional, spiritual and moral development of the whole child' (Hawkes, 2001). Teachers explain the meaning of the value, then pupils reflect on it and use the value to guide their actions over a period of time. As one ten year old expressed it:

> The way it works is – if the value was Friendship, if you're in the playground and you've fallen out with someone you think – it's Friendship – you're feeling bad and you'll make it up.
>
> *(Hawkes, 2001)*

The pupils have strong memories of certain values and what each one meant to them.

> The one which meant most to me was Understanding. I was going through a grumpy patch – it wasn't only that the other people understood me and what I was going through but I understood myself and that helped.
>
> When Tolerance was the value of the month I found that very helpful because I'm not very tolerant.
>
> *(Hawkes, 2001)*

On three mornings each week school assemblies introduce and explore the month's 'value' through readings, music and drama. Each half-hour assembly includes all 150 children and incorporates a significant period of stillness and silence. This appears to give a feeling of space to the whole day, allowing children a greatly enhanced experience of a balance of activities – active/passive; quiet/talking; communicating/reflective; taught skills/exploratory work.

Values education in Oxfordshire is supported by a resource pack produced by the council advisory service (Oxfordshire County Council, 2002). A letter accompanying the pack explains that the strategy arose from concern 'that pupil attitudes and behaviour are all too often negative and challenging. Such behaviour inhibits the development of a school ethos that both raises achievement and encourages pupils to be self-disciplined and develop holistically'. Values education is thus a preventive strategy to develop 'a vision for school effectiveness based on values and aims that will inspire a school's community'. One of the measures of the success of the programme at Stonesfield had been the reduced likelihood of children being excluded from the school.

7 Conclusion: towards universal provision

Fundamentally, all preventive upstream work develops because, and to the extent that, all those involved have been willing to listen and to learn from experience. This, as we have seen from the strategies explored in this unit, is almost invariably a complex process. The events leading up to a crisis or tragedy are often barely perceptible, but taken together they form the long 'chain of causation' referred to in public inquiries into, for example, the death of a child from abuse. On examination, the separate links in this chain reflect failures in a range of interconnected areas: obstructive legislation, organizational difficulties, inefficient use and/or lack of resources, inadequate communication (Roaf, 2002). Only a new, reframed and revitalized concept of 'community', equitably financed and supported by legislation, seems capable of unpicking this destructive chain and remaking it as a chain of prevention.

We have described how important the role of crisis and experience is in generating preventive strategies. We have also saluted the determined individuals, frequently unknown, who have used their downstream experience to develop upstream approaches and inclusive practice. The next unit explores the lessons of that experience more closely. Throughout both units, however, it is important to hold on to the idea that downstream and upstream are part of the same river.

References

Advisory Committee for Multi-cultural Education (ACME) (1982) *Education for Equality: a paper for discussion in Berkshire*, Reading, Berkshire County Council.

Anon (2002) 'Don't blame the young', letter to *The Guardian*, 29 April.

Association for Humanistic Psychology (2002) 'Humanistic psychology overview'. Available from: http://www.ahpweb.org/aboutahp/whatis.html (accessed September 2002).

Audit Commission (1992a) *Getting in on the Act. Provision for Pupils with Special Needs: the national picture*, London, HMSO.

Audit Commission (1992b) *Getting the Act Together. Provision for Pupils with Special Educational Needs*, London, HMSO.

Audit Commission (1994) *Seen But Not Heard: co-ordinating community child health and social services for children in need*, London, HMSO.

BBC (2000) 'Children in anti-smacking protest' Available from: http://news.bbc.co.uk/1/hi/uk/713992.stm (accessed December 2003).

BBC (2002) 'Mother jailed for girls" truancy'. Available from: http://news.bbc.co.uk/1/low/uk/1984502.stm (accessed January 2003).

BBC (2003) 'School meal changes bear fruit', 19 February 2003. Available from: http://news.bbc.co.uk/1/hi/scotland/2780089.stm (accessed December 2003).

Bennathan, M. and Boxall, M. (2000) *Effective Intervention in Primary Schools: nurture groups*, London, David Fulton.

Beresford, B. and Oldman, C. (2002) *Housing Matters: national evidence relating to disabled children and their housing*, London, JRF/ The Policy Press.

Bradshaw, J. (2002) 'Child poverty and child outcomes', *Children and Society*, **16**(2), pp. 131–40.

Burke, C. and Grosvenor, I. (2003) *The School I'd Like*, London, RoutledgeFalmer.

Butler-Sloss, Rt Hon. Justice E. (1988) *Report of the Inquiry into Child Abuse in Cleveland 1987*, Cm 412, London, HMSO.

Child Poverty Action Group (1999) 'School meals in Scotland: a CPAG briefing', October. Available from: http://www.cpag.org.uk/cro/Briefings/1099scotschmeals.htm (accessed December 2003).

Children and Young People's Unit (CYPU) (2001a) *Building a Strategy for Children and Young People: consultation document*, London, CYPU.

Children and Young People's Unit (CYPU) (2001b) *Tomorrow's Future: building a strategy for children and young people*, London, CYPU.

Collins, J., Harkin, J. and Nind, M. (2002) *Manifesto for Learning*, London, Continuum.

Connexions (2001) *Working with Connexions*, Nottingham, DfES Publications.

Cooper, P. and Lovey, J. (1999) 'Early intervention in emotional and behavioural difficulties: the role of nurture groups', *European Journal of Special Needs Education*, **14**(2), pp. 122–31.

Cremin, H. (2002) 'Pupils resolving disputes: successful peer mediation schemes share their secrets', *Support for Learning*, **17**(3), pp. 137–42.

Davies, J. D., Garner, P. and Lee, J. (1999) 'Special educational needs co-ordinators and the Code: no longer practising', *Support for Learning*, **14**(1), pp. 37–40.

Department for Education and Employment (DfEE) (1997) *Excellence in Schools*, London, DfEE (White Paper).

Department for Education and Skills (DfES) (2001) *Special Educational Needs Code of Practice*, London, DfES.

Department for Education and Skills (DfES) (2002) *Schools for the Future: Building Bulletin 95*, London, DfES.

Department for Education and Skills (DfES) (2003) *Working Together: giving children and young people a say*, London, DfES. Available from: http://www.dfes.gov.uk/consultations2/18/docs/ WORKING_TOGETHER.doc (accessed January 2003).

Department of Health (DoH) (1998) *Quality Protects: transforming children's services*. Available from: http://www.doh.gov.uk/scg/ quality.htm#intro (accessed December 2003).

Department of Health (DoH)/Department for Education and Employment (DfEE)/Home Office (2000) *Framework for the Assessment of Children in Need and their Families*, London, HMSO.

Department of Health (DoH)/Department for Education and Skills (DfES) (1998) *Our Healthier Nation*, London, DoH/DfES (Green Paper).

Department of Health (DoH)/Department for Education and Skills (DfES) and Welsh Office (1991) *Working Together: a guide to arrangements for inter-agency co-operation for the protection of children from abuse*, London, HMSO.

End Child Poverty (2002) *Tax and Benefits Briefing Paper*, London, End Child Poverty.

Foreign and Commonwealth Office (FCO) (2001) *Follow-up Report by the UK of Great Britain and Northern Ireland on its Implementation of the Goals of the 1990 World Summit for Children*, London, FCO.

Hart, S. (2000) *Thinking through Teaching*, London, David Fulton.

Harvey, R. (2002) 'A missed opportunity: reviewing the UN Special Summit on Children', *ChildRIGHT*, May, p. 186.

Hawkes, N. (2001) 'Being a school of excellence: "values-based education"'. Available from: http://www.livingvalues.net/reference/ excellence.htm/#Experience (accessed December 2003).

Hendey, N. and Pascall, G. (2002) *Disability and Transition to Adulthood: achieving independent living*, Brighton, JRF/Pavilion Publishing.

Holtermann, S. (1996) 'The impact of public expenditure and fiscal policies on Britain's children and young people', *Children and Society*, **10**(1), pp. 3–13.

Luxmoore, N. (2000) *Listening to Young People in School, Youth Work and Counselling*, London, Jessica Kingsley.

Maclagan, I. (2002) 'Making rights stick: Children's Rights Commissioner work in Oxfordshire', *Support for Learning*, **17**(3), pp. 132–6.

Meighan, R. (ed.) (1992) *Learning from Home-based Education*, Nottingham, Education Now.

Mitchell, D. E. and Scott, L. D. (1993) 'Professional and institutional perspectives on interagency collaboration' in *Politics of Education Association Yearbook 1993*, London, Falmer.

Moss, P. and Petrie, P. (1997) *Children's Services: time for a new approach*, London, Institute of Education, University of London.

Moss, P. and Petrie, P. (2002) *From Children's Services to Children's Spaces: public policy, children and childhood*, London, Routledge/ Falmer.

Neill, A. S. (1962) *Summerhill*, London, Gollancz.

O'Neill, O. (1986) *Faces of Hunger: an essay on poverty, justice and development*, London, Allen and Unwin.

Organisation for Economic Co-operation and Development (OECD) Centre for Educational Research and Innovation (1995) *Children and Youth at Risk* (draft), Paris, OECD.

Oxfordshire County Council (OCC) (2002) *Values Education: resource pack for primary schools*, Oxford, OCC Advisory and Improvement Service.

Payne, L. (2002) 'Children's rights and impact analysis: making children visible in government', *Support for Learning*, **17**(3), pp. 127–31.

Rahman, M., Palmer, G. and Kenway, P. (2001) *Monitoring Poverty and Social Exclusion 2001*, York, Joseph Rowntree Foundation.

Roaf, C. (1998) 'Interagency work in the management of inclusive education' in Clough, P. (1998) (ed.) *Managing Inclusive Education*, London, Paul Chapman.

Roaf, C. (2002) *Co-ordinating Services for Included Children*, Buckingham, Open University Press.

Spalding, B. (2000) 'The contribution of a "Quiet Place" to early intervention strategies for children with emotional and behavioural difficulties in mainstream schools', *British Journal of Special Education*, **27**(3), pp. 129–34.

Steiner, R., Parsons Whittaker, N. (trans.) and Lathe, R. (trans.) (1995) *The Spirit of the Waldorf School: lectures surrounding the founding of the first Waldorf school*, Stuttgart, Anthroposophic Press.

Swadener, B. B. and Lubeck, S. (eds) (1995) *Children and Families 'at Promise'*, Albany, State University of New York.

Thomas, G. and Loxley, A. (2001) *Deconstructing Special Education and Constructing Inclusion*, Buckingham, Open University Press.

Tomlinson, S. (1982) *A Sociology of Special Education*, London, Routledge and Kegan Paul.

UNESCO (United Nations Educational, Scientific and Cultural Organization) (1994) *The Salamanca Statement and Framework for Action on Special Needs Education*, Paris, UNESCO. Available from: http://www.unesco.org/education/information/nfsunesco/pdf/SALAMA_E.PDF (accessed September 2003).

UNICEF UK (1995) *The Convention on the Rights of the Child*, London, UNICEF.

Watson, C. and Marr, C. (2003) 'A breakfast club for children with emotional and behavioural difficulties', *Education 3–13*, October, pp. 15–18.

Wired for Health (2002) Healthy Schools Programme. Available from: http://www.wiredforhealth.gov.uk/healthy (accessed June 2002).

World Education Forum (2000) *The Dakar Framework for Action*, Paris, UNESCO.

Wright Mills, C. (1959) *The Sociological Imagination*, Oxford, Oxford University Press.

Yergin, D. and Stanislaw, J. (eds) (1998) *The Commanding Heights:* http://www.pbs.org/wgbh/commandingheights/shared/pdf/ess_britishwelfare.pdf (accessed July 2003).

Yule, W. and Gold, A. (1993) *Wise Before the Event: coping with crises in schools*, London, Calouste Gulbenkian Foundation.

UNIT 12 At the margins

Prepared for the course team by Melanie Nind, Caroline Roaf and Katy Simmons

Contents

1 Introduction

As we have explained, Units 11 and 12 together explore proactive and reactive measures to promote inclusion and prevent exclusion. These measures are often about preventing or responding to systemic barriers to inclusion and/or crises in the educational lives of children and young people. Some children and young people are hanging on to education by a thread – almost falling through the net of available support. For them, inclusion may be less about a seat in a mainstream classroom and more about maintaining any sort of link with education.

The learners at the margins covered in this unit are diverse. They could be said to have everything and nothing in common. They include Travellers, young people who truant, young offenders, and young people who are excluded and placed in pupil referral units, special provision or residential schools. We look at how students who are regarded as different are marginalized, such as asylum seekers and lesbian and gay young people. We describe measures to maintain education for pupils who are homeless or sick, who have mental health difficulties, or who are 'looked after' by local authorities. Some of these pupils are also disabled. We do not claim that the groups we look at include all those who may at some point experience marginalization. Other people might have a different list. Ofsted, for example, lists the following 'exclusion groups':

- girls and boys;

- minority ethnic and faith groups, Travellers, asylum seekers and refugees;

- pupils who need support to learn English as an additional language (EAL);

- pupils with special educational needs;

- gifted and talented pupils;

- children 'looked after' by the local authority;

- other children, such as sick children; young carers; those children from families under stress; pregnant school girls and teenage mothers; and any pupils who are at risk of disaffection and exclusion.

(Ofsted, 2000, p. 4)

Children and young people may find themselves at the margins of educational life after personal circumstances take their toll. Pressures on schools to raise standards and meet imposed targets have an impact, too, and create a climate in which excluding pupils can seem the only or best option for a school's overall viability. Students may oscillate between greater inclusion and exclusion at different times in their life and their school's life. However, structural inequalities in society mean that children and young people from some groups are more vulnerable than others. Proactive, upstream work is more likely to recognize and address these patterns of discrimination and structural inequalities. Reactive, downstream work, in contrast, is more likely to individualize the problem and the 'solution'.

Reactive measures may charitably attempt to rescue children from their situations. Voluntary organizations such as Include, the National Association for the Education of Sick Children and the Albert Kennedy Trust have certainly played key roles in raising the profile of children at the margins and in providing for them. Some of this work has been innovative and important and many of these organizations have understandably turned their attention to upstream work. Much of the reactive work to keep children connected to education goes on at local authority level, but some initiatives are national. Many schemes have not been evaluated formally and we encourage you to evaluate their contribution as you see it.

Learning outcomes

By the end of this unit you will:

- be able to identify some of the groups who are 'at the margins' of educational life and the processes that marginalize them;
- be able to identify some of the reactive measures and rescue schemes for these children and young people;
- be able to identify some key aspects of resilience that can assist children and young people to be 'survivors' rather than 'victims';
- further understand the relationship between preventive and reactive work in promoting inclusion and addressing exclusion.

Resources for the unit

For Activity 12.3, you will need to read:

- Chapter 12 in Reader 2, 'Interviews with young people about behavioural support: equality, fairness and rights' by Paul Hamill and Brian Boyd.

For Activity 12.4, you will need to read:

- Chapter 14 in Reader 2, 'Teachers and Gypsy Travellers' by Gwynedd Lloyd, Joan Stead, Elizabeth Jordan and Claire Norris.

You might also like to look at the following optional readings if you have the time or interest:

- Chapter 4 in Reader 2, 'Children's homes and school exclusion: redefining the problem' by Isabelle Brodie;
- Chapter 17 in Reader 2, 'Exclusion: a silent protest' by Janet Collins.

Next, we turn our attention to the issue of exclusion, starting with the formal act of *school exclusion* (formerly called 'expulsion' and known in Scotland as 'having an exclusion order issued'). In England and Wales, exclusions can be for fixed periods not exceeding 45 days in any one school year, or can be permanent (DfES, 2003a). We also explore the informal *social exclusion* that places some young people at the margins of educational life. Social exclusion is about more than physical presence: it is about facing barriers to participation in school and later in ordinary working life. This extends beyond the exclusion we have covered already in the course in relation to segregation in special schools. We ask who is excluded, how, and what happens to them then.

2 School exclusion

Who is excluded?

The population of excluded pupils includes an overwhelming over-representation of boys and Black students of African-Caribbean background who are five times more likely to be excluded than white pupils (Howson, 1998). Carl Parsons (1999a) reports that other minority ethnic groups are also excluded at higher rates than their presence in the population would lead one to expect, although Indian, Bangladeshi and Chinese pupils are exceptions to this pattern.

Despite government intervention, via the Social Exclusion Unit, to address disproportionate exclusion of Black students, the problem remains. Racist practices have not been eradicated and the stereotypes of the non-compliant African-Caribbean male and the compliant Asian pupil (Blyth and Milner, 1994) continue to affect exclusion practices. One parent explains how lack of cultural understanding plays a role:

> I think some teachers might think that black kids are more aggressive. There's cultural things. Black kids can be quite loud ... and sometimes that's interpreted as aggressiveness. It's about understanding the culture.
>
> (*African-Caribbean parent*)
>
> (*Osler* et al., 2002, p. 56)

Age and gender also help to determine who gets formally excluded, with two-thirds of exclusions being of pupils aged thirteen to fifteen (Howson, 1998); secondary school boys are four times more likely than girls to be excluded and primary school boys outnumber girls by fourteen to one. With girls amounting to only 17 per cent of permanent exclusions (DfEE, 2000), they have often been overlooked in prevention strategies and responses (Osler *et al.*, 2002). Much of girls' exclusion, however, is hidden as it is often unofficial social exclusion.

One might expect that if a pupil has a statement of special educational needs and is placed in (or excluded to) a special school, they will be protected from formal school exclusion, but this is not the case (Gross and McChrystal, 2001). In fact, Government statistics currently show that special schools have the highest rate of exclusions (DfES, 2003c, p. 5). Government figures (DfEE, 1999a) have shown the exclusion rate of pupils with statements to be seven times as high as that for pupils without statements. With regard to the wider population of children classified as having special educational needs (not just the minority who have statements), current official statistics show that they form two-thirds of the excluded population (DfES, 2003c, p. 91).

Social class is another dimension of inequality in relation to one's chances of being excluded. Children excluded from school are more likely to have experienced poverty, homelessness, parental illness and bereavement (Hayden, 1997). Most excluded pupils come from inner-city schools and start secondary school with a reading age behind that of their peers (Howson, 1998). A high proportion of young people in the criminal justice system are both excluded from schools and socially excluded.

People are not one-dimensional, and have several of these characteristics at once. For instance, the link between ethnicity and social class is relatively unexplored (Parsons, 1999a). Similarly, the way in which gender and race stereotypes combine to make success difficult and exclusion more likely for both African-Caribbean boys and girls needs examination: 'a greater proportion of Black girls [is] excluded than observed in any other ethnic group – in 2001/02 the rate of exclusion for Black girls is 3 times that for White girls. The exclusion rate for Black boys is twice that for White boys' (DfES, 2003b, p. 9). Audrey Osler and her colleagues say this about research into exclusion:

> Analyses of the problem have tended to focus on one or another of the groups of children judged to be vulnerable to exclusion (specific ethnic minorities, those with statements of special educational need) leading to strategies which fail to recognize that, in practice, there may be considerable overlap between these categories. If effective remedies are to be found to the current high levels of school exclusion then researchers and policy-makers need to develop a more comprehensive analysis.
>
> *(Osler et al., 2000, cited in Osler et al., 2002, p. 20)*

Being 'cared for' by the local authority makes being excluded 10 to 80 times more likely according to different studies (Gold, 1999). The market economy in which schools are in competition with each other has arguably increased exclusion for disadvantaged children and especially those in local authority care (Blyth and Milner, 1996).

Children who are excluded may have unmet learning support needs or unmet mental health needs (Young Minds, 1999) and exclusion increases the risk of further mental health problems developing (Kurtz and Thornes, 2000). Temporary intensive support to pupils who are stressed, depressed or bereaved may, however, prevent their exclusion and later mental health problems (Mallon, 1998), but whether pupils get this depends on their ethnicity, gender, parents' attitudes, and even where they live.

Pupils in England and Wales perceived as having behavioural difficulties are far more likely to be excluded from school than pupils in Scotland and Northern Ireland, or in other countries in Western Europe. In France, Germany, Belgium, Holland and Denmark, the child's right to continuous full-time education is enshrined in the law, thus preventing exclusion (Parsons, 1999b). Headteachers wanting to remove a pupil must find, with parental agreement, another placement for them. In Scotland, young people may be excluded for more than temporary or conditional exclusions, but such a decision lies with the LEA not the school, and a senior education officer or educational psychologist will find alternative provision.

There are, then, patterns in who is excluded, but there is also enormous variation from school to school. Pamela Munn, Gwynedd Lloyd and Mairi Ann Cullen (2000) studied exclusion and alternatives to exclusion and found that some schools exclude high numbers of pupils, some exclude for longer periods, and some exclude the same pupils repeatedly. Other schools have few or no official exclusions. Low excluding schools are more likely to have preventative approaches and strategies for maintaining pupils in school. They showed that although the 'social and economic status of pupils' had 'a profound effect on many aspects of school life, including attainment, truancy, discipline and staying on rates', this powerful influence was 'not sufficient as an explanation for different [exclusion] practices among schools' (Munn *et al.*, 2000, p. 29). A key explanatory factor was, in fact, school ethos: 'the beliefs of senior school staff about the purpose of schooling'. As one headteacher said:

> I think it is a moral thing, that you've got to say that those youngsters should be in education and it's education for all. It's not just education for the few that come in and don't cause us any problems.
>
> *(Munn et al., 2000, p. 52)*

Attempts to keep students in school

A major difference between low excluding and high excluding schools is upstream, proactive work. Schools succeed in avoiding formal exclusions by having networks of staff involved in decision making, such as pastoral care teachers, behaviour support staff, educational psychologists and senior managers. Here discipline and pastoral work are not divorced and the staff pull together at times of crisis for students.

In addition to, or instead of, proactive measures, schools also keep children in school through various interventions at times of difficulty. Some such interventions have resulted from the government Alternatives to Exclusion Grant Scheme. The KWESI project in Birmingham, for example, involved Black men supporting and mentoring African-Caribbean boys. The exclusion rates fell by 23 per cent with two-thirds of the reduction comprising minority ethnic pupils (Osler and Hill, 1999).

Exclusion from school or exclusion within school?

In an attempt to meet its targets for reducing exclusion the government invested in on-site units in what can be seen as a form of internal exclusion. This means that young people are not just excluded *from* school, but *within* school. The units were intended to enable children to follow individualized behaviour plans still ostensibly within their own schools but kept apart from their peers in ordinary classes. These were widely referred to in the press at the time of their announcement as 'sin-bins' (*Times Educational Supplement*, 24 April 2000). As Chris Searle (2001) discusses, such moves to isolate difficult children, who were predominantly Black, were seen by some as 'virtual ethnic cleansing'.

Susan Hallam and Frances Castle's evaluation of 'in-school centres' was more positive, though it revealed great variation in how the centres were implemented (Hallam and Castle, 2001). Centres successful in reducing exclusions provided a physical centre where staff were based and where pupils could go or be withdrawn to; had a strong commitment from senior management and other school staff; involved parents; and engaged pupils in self-monitoring. One pupil commented: 'If you think you need help you go and find [it]' (Hallam and Castle, 2001, p. 176).

Other forms of internal exclusion are more informal. Some schools succeed in avoiding the official exclusion of students by using alternative sanctions such as unofficially sending children home, unofficially agreeing part-time attendance and internal exclusion.

Activity 12.1

Read through the following examples and, if possible, discuss them with others, reflecting on the following issues:

(a)   Have these responses to troubled and troublesome students helped to keep them in mainstream education in the short term?

(b)   What about in the long term?

(c)   Is the students' continued inclusion more than superficial?

(d)   What alternative responses might schools have made?

(e)   What upstream, proactive work might have avoided the necessity to react at all?

We've made the agreement that ... I get home from work at 1.30 and if [my son] has had a bad morning, I just collect him then. [The headteacher] could quite easily suspend [i.e. exclude] him for things he's done in the last few weeks, but she's not because she knows it would interfere with my work ... There's nobody else to watch [look after] him.

(Mrs P., parent, in Munn *et al.*, 2000, p. 72)

They reckoned that she wasn't ready for full-time in school so I let it go for a wee while. Then [she] started getting a bit annoyed about it herself, asking '[Why] am I the only one getting taken out of class at dinner time and not getting to go back?' So I told her that she had to learn to behave herself and things like that. I think myself that she should have been allowed in a lot earlier than she was.

(Mr R., parent, in Munn *et al.*, 2000, pp. 72–3)

If there's a lot of motion or things going on where you can't supervise him all the time, we tend to exclude him [from those activities] and give him more set work. It tends to be quite easy work ... pitched just below his level so he can actually work through [it] and get a sense of achievement from finishing something.

(Class teacher in Munn *et al.*, 2000, p. 74)

 In the first example the parent clearly feels supported by the school; the family are not pushed further into crisis by the school's response. Moreover, the pupil is protected from the potential damage of the label and reputation that come with repeated exclusions. But this pupil is also being denied both schooling and access to real support to address his difficulties in the long term. The practice of sending the pupil home without officially recording it also helps the school (illegally) to keep down its exclusion figures.

In the second example, the parent and child feel less supported and involved in the decision making and again, the child is being excluded from a lot of her school experience. Because this is not a formal arrangement, however, the parent has no right of appeal.

The third example of internal exclusion is very common and represents considerable hours of lost or unbalanced curriculum experience. For some children, this might be time spent on other work and the difficulty of catching up with the work missed. For others, it might mean time spent sitting in corridors or the headteacher's office. It is a compromise teachers employ to allow other children to work and themselves to cope, whilst keeping the child linked and partially involved with their own class. Whether it is a compromise we would all find acceptable is, of course, questionable.

• • • • • • • • • • • • • • • • • • • •

Osler *et al.* (2002) found that girls are more likely to experience these kinds of internal exclusion, as well as self-exclusion through truanting, than they are to experience formal exclusion. Girls' invisibility in exclusion statistics and debates means they are not a priority in schools' thinking and have difficulty accessing help and services. This illustrates how informal exclusions can infringe rights.

As we saw in Unit 10, support classes, units or bases can also be a compromise or partial response to including some pupils. For pupils who might otherwise be excluded, such provision can allow for respite and support for all or some parties, while the pupils retain access to the mainstream environment and curriculum. How much these pupils experience curricular and social marginalization depends on a range of complex factors including the unit's location in relation to the main school, how much unit and mainstream staff work together, how much responsibility ordinary teachers retain for the pupils, and how much decision-making control pupils have.

Human resources

Another intervention found by Hallam and Castle (2001) to help reduce school exclusions (though there was no guarantee of this) was action by multi-disciplinary behaviour support teams. These teams are made up of educational psychologists, education welfare officers, social workers and specialist teachers. However, keeping students in school, whether or not they are in special bases or units, is more usually the job of teaching assistants and support teachers. These may be seen as 'behaviour supporters' as much as 'learning supporters' (see Unit 8).

Also vital are students' families. Munn *et al.* (2000) found that involving parents was the most common strategy to sustain pupils in school. This took forms ranging from parents signing behaviour-monitoring sheets, to taking part in multi-professional meetings, problem solving and action planning. Home visiting helped with building relationships and reciprocal support. Parental support for the approach deemed appropriate by the school was found to be a big factor in whether or not a pupil was excluded.

Mentors also form a rich source of support, as in the East London Schools School Home Support Scheme (Osler *et al.*, 2002), and in the mentoring role played by the joint assessment team social worker in Scotland. In the Excellence in Cities initiative, which targets individual pupils in inner-city schools, the role of mentors is to:

- transfer information, particularly at times of transition;
- co-ordinate support for particular individuals;
- draw up and implement action plans for individual pupils;
- maintain contact with families;
- act as a single point of contact for pupils accessing a number of services;
- work with voluntary mentors;
- work closely with parents.

(DfEE, 2002)

Mentors or individual supporters are often a key point of communication between pupil, parent, mainstream and specialist staff. They build trust so that all parties engage positively in the project of keeping the pupil participating in school life.

We can see the impact of an individual support teacher in one student's personal account:

> So I turned up and I was sitting there going 'I cannae do it, I cannae do it', but Sophia she was fabulous she gave me a great pushing and I really did work hard in the learning support and I caught up with all my work. Considering that I missed near enough three, four years of school while I was here, there and everywhere, she really did help me quite a bit because I got better grades in my exams than some of the other kids who had been there every day. So it's Sophia I've got to thank. She was really brilliant and there were a number of time when I just couldn't take it and she always gave me another chance.

(Lloyd and O'Regan, 1999, p. 42)

Peers too can be a source of great support and group work intervention can make use of this. One of the schools in Munn *et al.*'s (2000) research ran an 'adventure service team' scheme combining 60 per cent referred young people and 40 per cent 'average kids' to do 'solution-focused intervention' (Rhodes and Amjal, 1995). The scheme sought to use and build the young people's strengths so they would have less need to gain kudos in negative ways.

Individual exclusions can also be prevented with counselling and through teaching specific survival skills. Anger management training and conflict resolution schemes (Sharp and Cowie, 1998) have also been used with some success. The danger of these approaches is, though, that the problems are individualized and divorced from structural inequalities. The solutions are also seen as separate from any need to review the whole experience offered by schools. You might like to think about how an effective response might attack both angles. For example, we might offer a space for young people to go to when they need to calm down, while at the same time working to make ordinary classrooms less stressful. This could prevent damage both to class relationships and to pupils' own self-esteem.

What next after exclusion?

Exclusion from school is closely linked to later social exclusion. Excluded pupils tend to have poor employment and life prospects (DfEE, 2000; Social Exclusion Unit, 2001; Osler *et al.*, 2002). The path to this varies.

In England and Wales, pupils excluded following challenging behaviour are frequently placed in pupil referral units (PRUs) (these units do not exist in Scotland). PRUs were a response to the 1993 Education Act duty placed on LEAs to make educational provision for pupils out of school. Until 2002, there was no requirement for this provision to be full-time education and PRU placements were usually part-time. PRUs are not required to provide the national curriculum but they are required to offer a 'balanced and broadly based curriculum'.

PRUs are intended to give relatively short-term, off-site support to pupils, the majority catering only for pupils of secondary school age. Numbers on roll vary from single figures to over 100. While the Government does not see them as long-term alternatives to mainstream or special schools (DfEE, 1999b), Peter Gray and Sue Panter (2000) argue that this 'revolving door' idea of PRUs, where pupils re-enter mainstream after a brief spell, is simplistic and not matched by reality.

Evaluation of the effectiveness of PRUs has shown great variability in quality (Ofsted, 1999) with academic attainments of 'almost all' pupils found to be 'below national expectations', attendance often poor, and some PRUs having inadequate accommodation and resources. Such inadequacies may well impact on life chances.

Further, an Audit Commission report (1999) showed that getting a place in a PRU can be a very slow process once a pupil has been excluded from school. One unidentified council was taking an average of 18 weeks to provide alternative education for excluded pupils. A third of councils could not trace the whereabouts of excluded pupils six months after the end of the academic year during which they were excluded. Other research has shown that particular groups have difficulties even gaining placement in PRUs and girls may be sent to out-of-county residential schools (Rathbone CI, 1999).

Instead of being placed in PRUs, excluded pupils can be sent to other schools (mainstream, special or residential), further education colleges, secure and psychiatric units and offered home tuition (DfEE, 1999b). Most children out of school on short, temporary exclusions are not offered any alternative education. This becomes more of a problem as exclusions become longer or more frequent. Occasionally, and disastrously, young people are 'lost from the educational system down the gaps and cracks in the provision of alternative education' (Mitchell, 1996 quoted in Munn *et al.*, 2000, p. 114).

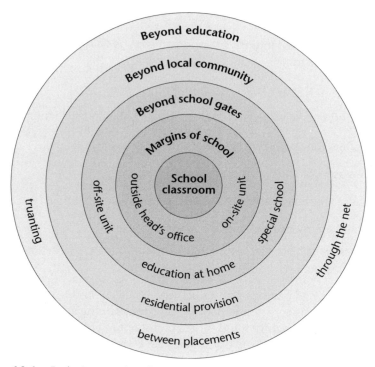

Figure 12.1   Exclusion to where?

Activity 12.2

How would you judge the effectiveness and appropriateness of provision for young people on the margins because of exclusionary processes related to their behaviour? Consider the following criteria and try to rank them in order of importance. If you can, compare and discuss your response with another student.

A   It allows other children to continue their work in a safe and orderly environment.   ☐

B   The decision making leading to the provision actively involves the young person.   ☐

C   The decision making leading to the provision actively involves the young person's parents.   ☐

D   It is the least intrusive option and maintains the strongest link with the original class/school/community.   ☐

E   It infringes the rights of the young person least.   ☐

F   It gives the most intensive support to change things for the young person.   ☐

G   It leads to the quickest re-inclusion of the pupil.   ☐

H   It offers the fullest access to a broad and balanced curriculum.   ☐

J   It offers the best value for money   ☐

K   The users of the provision evaluate it highly.   ☐

L   There are measurable educational outcomes.   ☐

M   There are measurable behavioural outcomes.   ☐

You may well have found this activity difficult as there are no right or wrong answers. Some people focus more on rights, some on measurable outcomes and others on retaining links with the mainstream. Part of the purpose of the activity is to raise questions about the aims of provision for pupils at the margins. We cannot know if provision is effective unless we are clear about what it is meant to do for young people. There is a tension between the need to remove troubled/troublesome pupils for the benefit of other pupils' learning and the needs and rights of the person deemed to be troubled/troublesome. We need to be guided in our thinking by key principles and it can be helpful to remind ourselves of the social model of disability and the rights debates, which prompt us to focus on societal barriers rather than individual problems.

* *

The impact of exclusion

The impact of exclusion on pupils and their families is considerable. Munn *et al.* (2000) sum up the range of feelings experienced by pupils, from the immediate strong feelings of rejection, fear and injustice, to the long-term fear about the effects of the exclusion. They note angry reactions experienced at home, boredom and acquisition of a negative reputation while the young people miss school. Excluded pupils talked about a sense of injustice in their treatment:

> If they're going to chuck me out for something I deserve to get chucked out for, then fair enough. I didn't think I deserved to get chucked out because I didn't do a punishment exercise. It's different if you have been fighting or if you've been causing trouble in the class.
>
> *(Jean A. in Munn et al., 2000, p. 3)*

Exclusions can lead to parents feeling they have to punish their children further, sometimes with further exclusions from friends, aspects of family life or even the home. Crisis, the charity working with homeless people, reported that a quarter of those living rough had been excluded from school (Ghouri, 1999).

Even temporary exclusions can lead to great difficulties in returning to school, in terms of both catching up with school work and mixing with peers. They can also cause problems later with finding work, as one boy explains:

> When I'm getting a job, people will look at my records and things like that and they might not employ me because I've been suspended ... They think you could swear at an employee or something like that or could end up hitting them or swear at a customer or something like that. 'He can't control his temper.'
>
> *(Wayne T. in Munn et al., 2000, p. 8)*

These personal accounts of what it means to be excluded from school are important reminders of the need for proactive work to avoid such situations. As conceded in the Ofsted report *Exclusions from Secondary Schools*, 'no democracy can afford to write off thousands of young people' (Ofsted, 1996). Yet there is strong evidence of the links between exclusion and subsequent problems in later life, such as prisoners being over twenty times more likely than the general population to have been excluded from school (SEU, 2002).

◯ Activity 12.3

Now read Chapter 12 in Reader 2, 'Interviews with young people about behavioural support: equality, fairness and rights' by Paul Hamill and Brian Boyd.

What can pupils tell us about how to respond to, or prevent, disaffection?

Make a note in your learning journal of the ways in which pupils' views were sought. This will help you with your final assignment in which you will seek the views of someone in a different position or with a different perspective from your own.

3 Exclusion from the local community

Living away from home

The route to residential school may be via the kinds of formal exclusion we have talked about, but for disabled children the process of exclusion may be subtler. The discourse of meeting need may disguise the fact that children are being excluded from their local schools. The residential school option is often 'necessitated' by inadequate upstream work, as explained by one senior education officer:

> The problem with the Out of County Placements Panel is that we're picking up problems too late, e.g. five or six times a year we get a child referred, in a local SLD school or mainstream, doing reasonably well at school but the parents can't cope, respite is inadequate, and as a result education is beginning to unravel. This all leads to a request for a residential placement. If there is good parenting, and good respite care, the child's needs could be met in county. But if we know that things are going wrong, what can we do? If we'd got around that child's problems earlier, planned for support to parents, psychiatric input, etc., we could have kept the child at home within Children Act principles.
>
> *(Morris, 1998b, pp. 79–80)*

You will be able to note a mixture of blaming the child, the parent and/or the environment in this comment. In circumstances like these, education officers often talk of education bailing out social services because education and social services departments are not working together.

The experiences of children and young people

Placement at a residential school can mean that children and young people are at the heart of new educational lives with a strong network of friends, while being at the margins of family and community life. Jenny Morris (1998a) asked disabled youngsters living away from home about their experiences. One student, Keith explains:

> I had them [my family] in my head but I sort of blocked them out. When I was at school I blocked my family out of me so I didn't get emotional and so all my energy was within that school. I totally forgot about the family while I was at school, that's how I managed.
>
> *(Morris, 1998a, p. 7)*

Keith talks about survival strategies and also about being bored and disorientated when he went home in the holidays. Howard, another student, moved to boarding school after his school and family experienced difficulties with his behaviour. His school in the country housed 200 children and smelled and looked like an institution. He was the only African-Caribbean person there and isolated from his cultural community. Ayesha Vernon recalls her experience of such isolation:

> My experience of racism started when I went to my first residential school for the blind which was all white apart from myself and an Asian boy. There I experienced physical and verbal abuse from the children and less favourable treatment from some of the staff. I could hardly speak any English, I wore Indian clothes and as a Muslim I needed a special diet. Gradually and in subtle ways, I was persuaded to wear English clothes and eat English food.
>
> *(Vernon, 1996, p. 50)*

Some of the children in Morris's study liked their residential placement and others did not, depending partly on whether they made friends and how they felt about the decision to go there. Lenny described how his mother couldn't control him and ended up becoming violent towards him and his siblings. He talked about his mixed feelings about being sent away and his trying to make sense of the reasons why:

> I'm resentful towards my mum because I was in a wheelchair and I was the one that had to come here ... for one day I would think it was because I was in a wheelchair, for another day I thought it was because I'm the only black kid that my mum's got ... it could have been, it could have been. But now I feel I was very silly for thinking like that, because it has nothing to do with my colour it was more to do with that she was having babies

... It could have been because I was in a wheelchair, it was very hard, very hard especially when I was growing up because if my mum left me in the house, I used to crawl out the door, crawl over the road risking life and limb like. She was worried sick.

(Morris, 1998a, pp. 13–14)

Respite

The build-up to a move to residential school or public care (children's homes or foster placements) may be protracted and difficult. One intervention aimed at preventing this conclusion is 'respite care', a form of crisis management that gives families a short break or series of short breaks from the challenge of caring for their child. Jenny Morris (1998b, p. 10) is one of many disabled people who objects to the term 'respite care' 'because it implies that there is a need for relief from a burden, and that the burden is the disabled person'. Respite or short breaks may have a preventative element in working to retain children in their family homes and communities in the longer term, but the provision is more often a reactive measure made only when crisis has occurred. Indeed, Jenny Morris (1998b) found that some local authorities *only* provided crisis services and not the flexible, low-key support that parents wanted. Ronny Flynn (2002) found that Black and Asian families experienced considerable barriers to accessing breaks to support children and their families, including the myth that they have their own effective support networks and don't want outside interference, when what they want is individually and culturally sensitive support. Just as school exclusions highlight the tensions between individual and class group needs, respite care breaks highlight the tensions between individual and family needs. Family needs rather than the needs and perspectives of the young person can often drive the provision, which may feel like a punishment if not adequately explained and planned. Much more is known about what services families want than about what the young people themselves want and feel (Morris, 1998b).

In best practice, however, the views of all concerned are heard and a response made accordingly. Jenny Morris (1998b) reports one such example in which a parent sought a break from looking after her teenager daughter. The response made by the voluntary organization to this *and* the daughter's need was to enable her to spend an evening a week with other disabled youngsters by providing a venue and transport. The group planned and undertook, with volunteers, their own weekend away. Such flexibility and responsiveness, however, is rare.

4   Non-attendance

We now turn to a different aspect of marginalization: children and young people who to some extent can be said to exclude themselves through non-attendance. Officially, pupils' absence is recorded as authorized, that is condoned by parents, or unauthorized. As will become clear, however, whatever the nature of the absence, non-attending children and young people are by no means a homogeneous group.

Who truants and why?

Truants tend to be older students and from poorer backgrounds.

Pupils who truant can be very much at the margins of educational life. They may not be marginalized when they start truanting, but become so through the accumulation of the effects of truanting. Much may depend on whether they are already marginalized in some way, and, as with exclusion, the population of young people who truant does not match the wider school community. Studies reported by the Social Exclusion Unit (SEU) confirm that truants tend to be older students and from poorer backgrounds. Parents of truants are more likely to be in low-skilled than professional or managerial jobs and more likely to be in local authority housing than owner-occupiers (SEU, 1998). For boys, living in a single-parent family appears to be a risk factor. Interestingly, other groups that show up disproportionately in school exclusions (notably pupils from some minority ethnic groups) are not more likely to be persistent truants.

Eric Blyth and Judith Milner (1987) argue that pupils who truant are pupils who find school irrelevant or even humiliating, making their truanting a rational response. Carl Parsons (1999a) describes this as pupils voting with their feet. Frequent reasons given by young people for not going to school are bullying, difficulties with lessons, feeling a failure and home problems, whereas the reasons for attending school are meeting friends, learning new things, achieving success and pleasing parents (Quality in Education Centre, 1995). It is easy to see how some young people weigh incentives and disincentives and decide in favour of not attending.

Osler *et al.* (2002) found that for girls self-exclusion is a strategy for dealing with friendship and other difficulties at school, including bullying which, because it is protracted, verbal and psychological in nature, is often not recognized or dealt with by schools. As these girls explained:

> If a boy's going to bully he'll use violence. Girls do it mentally because they're clever. They know it hurts more.
>
> (*Michelle, year 11, mainstream school, no exclusions*)
>
> [...]
>
> I was bullied at this school for three years ... and the teachers ... I did go to them and my parents as well ... and, like, it helped a bit, but they couldn't suspend 'er or nothing 'cause she hadn't physically touched me but to me, it wasn't about what she was doing physically ... she was just destroying me mentally.
>
> (*Nina, year 11, mainstream school, fixed-term excluded*)
>
> And I was getting called fat and everything and then [other pupils] they'd mostly swear at me and ... it was just stupid but it really got on my nerves so I didn't want to go.
>
> (*Emma, year 11, long-term non-attender, now at FE college*)
>
> (*Osler* et al., *2002, pp. 39–40*)

In practice, only some students who truant find themselves labelled or regarded as 'truants'. Much depends on cultural and professional attitudes. School phobia provides a medically certifiable justification for absence from school (and exempts parents from prosecution: see Blagg, 1987). In Felicity Armstrong's interviews with teachers about truancy, one teacher described the very different ways in which two primary school pupils were regarded in the same school, on the advice of the same educational psychologist:

> One boy was treated with great sensitivity by the teachers at the school and by the educational psychologist. It was decided that he was suffering from 'school phobia' and was allowed to arrive after the other children and attend lessons if he felt able to. If he preferred he could read or work in the school library. He was referred to a psychiatric

unit (by an educational psychologist) where he and his family received counselling.

(Open University, 2001, p. 37)

The other boy, of similar age (eleven), was 'physically dragged' to his desk in front of his class. The teacher explains:

> The same educational psychologist saw this boy. He did not refer him for any special help. He explained the legal position to the mother who became increasingly terrified she would be taken to court and her son would be 'put in a home' or she would be fined. This boy was seen as a 'truant' and spoilt and manipulative. The parents of the first boy were college lecturers. The mother of the second boy was single and worked part-time in a shop.

(Open University, 2001, p. 38)

Both boys continued to have difficulty in attending school. Both of them said they hated school, but the professionals responded by finding problems located within the pupils rather than examining problems within the school: one case was seen as psychiatric and the other social/behavioural.

The outcome of truanting for young people

The outcome of truanting for young people depends somewhat on the extent to which they do it. Even with inconsistent truanting, lessons are missed, social relationships are altered and pupils can find themselves caught in a web of intervention to 'support' them. Pupils' accounts of their experiences illustrate how an exclusionary process gathers momentum:

> I didn't really fit in so I didn't want to go to school. Teachers wouldn't really help me with my work. It really started from there.
>
> [...]
>
> And then it's hard to come back ... you're behind with work ... can't catch up and it's easier to stay away.
>
> *(Stacy, year 11, PRU, long-term non-attender)*

(Osler et al., 2002, pp. 46–7)

The Elton Report (DES, 1989) recommended what we would see as upstream, proactive 'positive strategies' for improving attendance and 'alternative curriculum' approaches. Less proactive and more reactive, the Report also recommended the development of LEA behaviour support teams to work with truants. This was seen as a more inclusive alternative in preference to on or off-site 'units', so that mainstream teachers could develop skills in working with 'difficult' young people. Much stress, however, was placed on the close surveillance of students.

The Elton Report further recommended funding for 'innovative projects for meeting the needs of the most difficult pupils and their schools' (DES, 1989, p. 158). This resulted in a range of 'truancy watch' schemes and projects to reduce bullying, but few involving outside agencies, such as police, educational psychologists or youth workers, and even fewer addressing teaching methods or the curriculum. As we know, however, it is the curriculum that excludes many Black and working-class children:

> They are excluded by what they are commanded to learn and by much of the prescribed body of knowledge, which often relates to them only inasmuch as it humiliates and ignores them. They are frequently excluded by prevailing attitudes towards race, class, gender, language, history, religion, culture and the essential features of the communities to which they belong.
>
> *(Searle, 2001, p. 11)*

Care or control?

Responses to truancy have oscillated between controlling and caring policies, and the education welfare service sits uneasily between education and social work, though without the professional status of either. Before the 1990s, LEAs could also apply to the juvenile court under Section 1(2) of the 1969 Children and Young Person's Act for a young person to be taken into care because of their poor attendance, although a social work supervision order was the more common outcome. The 1989 Children Act (Schedule 3, Part III) curtailed LEAs' power to institute care proceedings and introduced education supervision orders, whereby education welfare officers were required to 'advise, assist and befriend and give directions to' a child and his or her parents to 'secure that' the child was 'properly educated'. The order remains in force for a year but can be extended by the court for up to three years. It is still possible for absence from school to be considered as a reason for care proceedings to be brought by a social services department if it is considered that a young person is out of parental control or at risk of physical or psychological harm. In Scotland, children's hearings make recommendations, sometimes for placement in a residential school for young offenders.

From the 1950s to the 1980s, pupils' welfare was increasingly emphasized in discussions of interventions, but since then governments have stressed punishment for parents and a direct attack on school attendance. Currently (2003) parents who fail to ensure that their children are in full-time education can be fined and imprisoned after a third conviction. 2002 saw the first imprisonment of a parent for her child's failure to attend school.

Criminalization is also an issue when 'whether officially or unofficially excluded, children who reject education because it appears to be rejecting them ... become involved in crime and further trouble, both in and out of school' (Searle, 2001, p. 3). This led local authorities such as Sheffield to adopt anti-truancy task forces, in which police and council truancy officers 'round up' children from the streets.

Cullen *et al.* (1996) have evaluated provision in England and Scotland for children who truant and found that some pupils did not attend the programmes, continued to be disruptive or were not interested in what was on offer. However, the main reason for this was 'programmes that did not match their interests or aptitudes and that were not relevant to the young people's aspirations for their future' (Cullen *et al.*, 2000, p. 3). Programmes judged 'effective' were based on 'the interests, aptitudes and aspirations of individual young people'. When 'well planned, run and monitored, these programmes could be an effective way of enabling pupils to move into positive progression routes post-

16. They succeeded in re-engaging and re-motivating previously disaffected and disengaged young people' (Cullen *et al.*, 2000).

5 Excluded by the back door

Intermittent school attendance

Formal exclusion and truanting are not the only ways in which pupils are cut off from full-time education and the full curriculum. The head of a project for pregnant teenagers describes a different process:

> The problem with pregnant girls is not formal exclusion but informal exclusion like sporadic attendance, school moves and home tuition: pregnant girls are excluded by the back door.
>
> *(Osler et al., 2002, pp. 61–2)*

Travellers, children and young people who are ill, 'looked after' by local authorities, homeless, living in poverty, or even perhaps educated at home, may also experience loss of educational opportunity and involvement. Pupils are sometimes out of school during disputes about special or mainstream placements. Some young people, such as lesbian and gay young people and asylum seekers, are also cast as deviants, further marginalizing them.

Exclusionary processes and Travellers

Travellers may be at the margins of educational life because of their intermittent patterns of school attendance. This may be true of children with health problems too, but they are generally seen as more 'deserving' of support (Jordan, 2001) (although, as we will see later, much depends on the type of illness). Discontinuity of school experience contributes to Traveller pupils' underachievement and exclusion (Jordan, 1996) and notions of being undeserving stem from notions that 'they have brought this on for themselves'. Thus, the educational issues related to attendance patterns may be constructed as the Traveller pupils' problem and not the schools'.

Issues to do with attendance patterns, however, are only part of the story for Travellers. Gwynedd Lloyd and colleagues examined the various exclusionary processes at work in the school experiences of Gypsy Traveller children in Scotland.

Activity 12.4

Now read Chapter 14 in Reader 2, 'Teachers and Gypsy Travellers' by Gwynedd Lloyd, Joan Stead, Elizabeth Jordan and Claire Norris.

(a)   Make a note of the exclusionary processes that are revealed through the interviews with the teachers.

(b)   Then try to articulate for yourself in your own words, out loud or on paper, the complex interaction of factors that leave Traveller pupils at the margins of formal educational life.

Gypsy Travellers are a minority ethnic group who, like other groups whose cultural differences are not valued, experience discrimination and oppression. Racism and bullying contribute towards Traveller children feeling marginalized and excluded from state education. Pressures to conform and be 'normalized' act against the children in two ways. Firstly, Gypsy Traveller pupils break explicit rules by fighting back against name-calling, being late to classes and so on, which can lead to formal exclusion. Secondly, they break unspoken rules by not acting out the role of pupil as required by the subtle pressures of school life, which leads to informal exclusion. As Lloyd *et al.* explain, Gypsy Travellers pose a threat because they resist assimilation and instead take what they require from education to survive.

As the chapter explains, Gypsy Traveller pupils participate less as they get older. They very rarely go on to further or higher education, but there have been examples of this following positive intervention. Work is being done to address Travellers' curricular/school experiences to make them more inclusive by explicitly welcoming this aspect of diversity. But there are also schemes that Elizabeth Jordan (2001) describes that respond both to the needs to Traveller pupils in school and to the issue of their intermittent attendance. These projects use information technology to allow pupils to stay in direct contact with their base schools while travelling. The projects are innovative and more evaluation is needed, but the indications are that such flexible and technological support can enable highly mobile pupils to maintain some momentum with their schoolwork. Crucially, the fact that the schemes raise scholastic achievement by changing aspects of the school system that are ordinarily exclusionary also helps to make pupils feel valued.

Lack of focused thought: sick children

Alison Closs (2000b) describes the educational problems experienced by sick children as absence, under-performance while feeling under par, disruption because of treatment, peer rejection and uncertain futures. In addition, many sick children are also already part of a disadvantaged group – disabled or in poverty. For sick children, longer-term conditions have longer-term effects, but the effects of intermittent illness can be cumulative and serious. Official figures estimate that 'in any given year there are some 100,000 children and young people who require education outside school because of illness or injury. In addition there are a significant number of children and young people who experience clinically defined mental health problems' (DfES, 2003d). However, as Alison Closs argues, it is actually a 'lack of focused thought on the part of education providers and lack of preparedness to ensure quality education, rather than actual medical conditions, that put children's education most at risk' (Closs, 2000b, p. 4).

With appropriate upstream measures ordinary schools often cope with the diverse needs of children with health difficulties. However, because only some of them are deemed by legislation to have 'special educational needs' or to be disabled, many fall through the net of available support (Closs, 2000b).

Sick pupils are generally considered deserving of care and consideration in education, with, as Alison Closs notes, some exceptions:

> Just as Sally Tomlinson (1982) famously described every mainstream school's most and least favoured potential pupil with special educational needs (a bright little girl in a wheelchair and a dull disruptive boy) nearly 20 years ago, so a competitor for the dull and disruptive child has now emerged. He or she may be doubly incontinent, may require catheterization of urine, may need rectal suppositories or injections.
>
> *(Closs, 2000b, p.13)*

It is people's attitudes, and not the surmountable practical problems, which push this child to the margins. Support for such sick pupils is seen more as a matter of benevolence than rights, making them vulnerable to the vagaries of *ad hoc* arrangements. Nonetheless, many of the interventions that sustain the participation of young people whose behaviour is challenging or who truant work equally well for sick children. One first-person account illustrates this:

> My school had a facility called 'The Base' for pupils who needed to work out of their usual class for a variety of reasons. This meant that on days when I was not feeling well I could go there and work quietly at my own pace.

I certainly wouldn't have been at school half as much
without 'The Base'. I became very friendly with one of the
teachers who worked there. She provided not only
educational support, but emotional support as well.

(Hegarty et al., 2000, pp. 15–16)

When the boundaries between wellness and illness are not clear-cut,
such as in the intermittent ill-health experienced by pupils with ME,
deservedness may be doubted and understanding lacking (Closs and
Norris, 1997). Even when pupils are considered to deserve support and
their absence is authorized, Closs (2000a) argues that they are rarely a
priority. Even though authorized absence from school is far more
extensive than unauthorized absence, there are practical, ethical and
attitudinal barriers to confronting the problem:

There are, of course, many competing heavy demands on
education staff's time and thought. A quiet,
intermittently absent and debatably poorly population,
probably assumed to be safe in bed rather than involved
in crime when absent, are not in an obviously strongly
competitive situation for attention.

(Closs, 2000a, p. 136)

Stigma and underachievement: 'looked after' children

Children in care are no more homogeneous a group than any other.
Disabled children and children from minority ethnic backgrounds,
though, are over-represented in the in-care population (DfEE/DoH,
2000, paras 4.18 and 4.21) and the proportion of younger children is
growing (DfEE/DoH, 2000, para. 3.1).

In 2000, in a publication called *Guidance on the Education of Children
and Young People in Public Care*, the Departments of Education and
Health explained why children were in public care, were looked after
by local authorities and who they were:

Children enter public care for a variety of reasons. Many
will have been affected by distressing and damaging
experiences, including physical and sexual abuse and
neglect. Some will be in public care because of the illness
or death of a parent or because their families are in some
way unable to provide adequate care for them. The
majority of young people in public care come from
families who experience hardship and are separated from
them because of some form of family upheaval or
breakdown. Less than two per cent of young people are in
public care because of offences they have committed.

(DfEE/DoH, 2000, para. 3.4)

Children in care may be marginalized in school because of the stigma
and low expectations associated with their living situation. They also

have to cope with discontinuity in their home and school lives. Changes of school may be sudden or finding new schools after changes in accommodation may be delayed. Many children return home after a considerable period away but return to their local school is not easy, particularly for adolescents returning to secondary schools which are not child-centred (Bullock, Little and Millham, 1994). One adolescent commented: 'Everyone just asked questions. Because you'd been in a children's home they thought you were criminal, they asked "What did you do?", "How much did you nick?", "Did you try to kill someone?"' (Bullock and Little, 1994, p. 308).

Planned breaks and organized returns are less problematic than the sudden arrival of highly mobile pupils. These youngsters 'have usually been irregular attendees and have been ostracised by peers beforehand' and so are made to feel unwelcome on return. Children may then experience bullying, racial abuse and harassment, yet schools do not always consider the young person's social network as crucial to their re-settlement. Children and young people in public care have greatly increased rates of mental health problems (Mental Health Foundation, 1999).

The fragmented nature of education for children in care means they often experience difficulty in making and sustaining friendships and they seriously underachieve (DfEE/DH, 2000). Over 75 per cent of care leavers have no educational qualifications at all and only 3 per cent achieve five GCSEs at grade C or above (compared to 60 per cent in the non-care population); less than 1 per cent enter higher education (Jackson and Martin, 1998).

It is only since 1990 that concerns about the welfare of children looked after by local authorities has extended to their educational careers (Jackson, 1994) and given rise to government interest in promoting better achievement. This has translated into various government-supported, local responses to the problem of underachievement.

 ## Activity 12.5

Review the following three examples of projects to support the education of children in public care. These are adapted from the DfEE/DoH guidance referred to above. Which of these would you rate most highly as inclusive education? Which is most proactive and preventative? Doing this activity will help you to formulate your own thinking on inclusive education, thus helping your work on your assignment.

1   Surrey LEA allocated an additional £500 per pupil in care per year to its secondary schools to help raise the profile of young people in care, to improve their education, and to provide opportunities for joint education and social service planning. They suggested schools used the funding to obtain four days' supply cover for the nominated teacher in school to for example: maintain a register of looked after pupils, liaise with social services, provide induction for new pupils, attend training.

2   Hampshire County Council's strategies for raising the attainments of young people in public care included a strategy for raising literacy levels. This involved setting literacy targets, homework clubs in children's homes, special summer schools for young people in care and additional books given to children's homes and foster carers.

3   The social services and education departments of a group of counties worked with the National Children's Bureau to develop multi-disciplinary groups at local authority level with the core aim of improving educational opportunities for children in care. This opened up dialogue about where the barriers were and led to trying out co-ordinated approaches and sharing best practice.

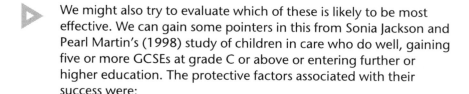

We might also try to evaluate which of these is likely to be most effective. We can gain some pointers in this from Sonia Jackson and Pearl Martin's (1998) study of children in care who do well, gaining five or more GCSEs at grade C or above or entering further or higher education. The protective factors associated with their success were:

(i)   stability and continuity;

(ii)   learning to read early and fluently;

(iii) having a parent or carer who valued education and saw it as the route to a good life;

(iv)   having friends outside care who did well at school;

(v)   developing out-of-school interests and hobbies;

(vi)   meeting a significant adult who offered consistent support and encouragement and acted as a mentor and possibly role model;

(vii) attending school regularly.

(Jackson and Martin, 1998, p. 578)

This indicates that interpersonal relationships with positively influential adults and early efforts to influence levels of literacy are likely to be effective, alongside interventions encouraging better attendance. A study of the educational attainment of children who are fostered (Heath, Colton and Aldgate, 1994) concluded that it is the intensity of intervention that makes a difference: 'greater-than-average progress needs greater-than-average inputs' (p. 257) and thus, 'the educational needs of separated children must be given much higher priority' (p. 258). Nonetheless, however good downstream work may be, this does not negate the fact that the structural issues of a failure of education and social services to collaborate has been a major factor in the educational difficulties of young people in care (Fletcher-Campbell and Hall, 1991; Jackson, 1994).

•   •   •   •   •   •   •   •   •   •   •   •   •   •   •   •   •   •   •   •

The government's own statutory guidance requires schools in England and Wales to designate teachers to advocate for young people in care and liaise with other services and to ensure that every young person in care has a Personal Education Plan (PEP). The PEP is intended to contribute to stability for the pupil by recording particular needs, achievements and targets. The PEP is an 'integral part of the Care Plan'; thus a pupil in care may have a Personal Education Plan, a Care Plan, an Individual Education Plan, a Statement of Special Educational Needs, a Careers Action Plan, a Pastoral Support Programme, and a Learning Mentor Action Plan (DfEE/DoH, 2000, para. 5.20). One might conclude that pupils who are the subjects of so much planning should not be at the margins of school life!

Refugee children

Traumatic life changes, stigma and underachievement are also experienced by refugee children. Neil Remsbery (2002), from the National Children's Bureau Pupil Inclusion Unit, has argued that while schools can play 'a vital role in restoring a sense of normality for young asylum seekers, whose lives have been disrupted by traumatic experiences ... they are often excluded from school because there are not enough spaces, or because they may have additional educational needs'. Moreover, they may be excluded because they are unwelcome and made a scapegoat for other problems of unmet need. Racist bullying and verbal and physical abuse of asylum seekers is common and increasing (Stanley, 2001).

Many refugee children are without a school place and finding one is particularly hard for fifteen year olds seeking a placement before they become sixteen (Rutter, 2001). The impact of new asylum-seeking fourteen and fifteen year olds on school league tables may be one reason for this. Disabled people in refugee and asylum-seeking communities in Britain have other unmet needs for social care, aids and equipment, housing and finance, and these disabling barriers and lack of social networks keep them at the margins and indeed often highly isolated (Roberts and Harris, 2002).

According to Lucy Clarke (2002), a project worker with the East Oxford Schools Inclusion Project, 'from a school's point of view' educating young people seeking asylum 'presents a daunting list of challenges'. Among these she lists interrupted schooling, depression and post-traumatic stress, and, for unaccompanied minors, the absence of family or indeed, any adult support.

> Add to this the pitfalls of the ever-changing asylum system accentuating youngsters' uncertainty about the length of their stay. Throw in inconsistent, and often inadequate housing and you can imagine why, despite very high motivation, young asylum seekers might find it difficult to concentrate on their school work. And why a school might be nervous about their arrival.
>
> *(Clarke, 2002)*

In some areas, local schools and communities have reacted positively, welcoming refugees and asylum seekers with practical support and imagination. In Oxford, local charities such as Asylum Welcome and Action for Children in Conflict provide practical support to the young people themselves as well to schools through training for volunteer mentors. At Villiers School in Southall a creative project emerged in the aftermath of the events of 11 September 2001. It began when Farid Ahmad, a young Afghan refugee,

> approached Dai Jones, assistant head teacher, because he wanted the chance to tell his stories, not just to the school but to a wider audience.
>
> It was then that Mr Jones realized that other students in the school also wanted the opportunity to tell their story. So he set up a project run by pupils Beshandeep Sehra, 14, and Katija Ali, 14, which gave refugee children the chance to articulate their equally tragic histories.
>
> *(Ward, 2001, p. 4)*

One outcome was a performance, in June 2002, in words, dance and music by the students to celebrate the refugee communities of the world. Ruvimbo Bungwe, 14, contributed this poem:

> So I have a new name, refugee. Strange that a name should take away from me my past, my personality and hope. Strange refuge this.
>
> So many seem to share this name, refugee, yet we share so many differences.
>
> I find no comfort in my new name. I long to share my past, restore my pride,

To show I, too, in time, will offer more
Than I have borrowed. For now, the comfort that I seek resides
in the old, yet new, name I would choose.
Friend.

(Bungwe, 2002)

Constructions of 'other': 'othering'

A useful critical concept in understanding the processes of marginalization is 'othering' (Shakespeare, 1994). In othering, some people are constructed as other to the majority norm. Thus concepts of what beautiful and healthy bodies should look like position disabled people as other, sexist assumptions position men centrally and women as other, ethnocentric assumptions position an array of diverse cultures as simply 'non-white'. Children and young people who do not conform are 'othered' by processes that label them as different. Nasa Begum describes this process at its least subtle:

> It took me a long time to understand why people who did not know me in my neighbourhood called me 'spastic', 'bandy legs' or 'Ironside' and why people with disabilities called me 'paki' or 'nigger'. Eventually I learned that wherever I went I would probably stand out as being different from the majority.

(Begum, 1994, p. 50)

In its more subtle form, othering labels people as having deficits, disorders, special needs. Transgressing rules or norms leads to their categorization as deviant. Through othering, some children and young people, and often their families with them, are made to seem less worthy, even less human.

Lesbian and gay young people

Sexual minority youth is a group that is marginalized through the process of othering. Sexuality does not interfere with learning, but a lack of recognition and value as a lesbian or gay young person and bullying and harassment do. Schools do not openly address the sexuality of lesbian and gay youth nor the threats they receive in response to it. This negates their identity and makes them vulnerable. Lack of support at school can compound lack of support at home and lead to both non-attendance and homelessness.

The Albert Kennedy Trust was set up following the death of sixteen-year-old Albert Kennedy:

> ... Albert fell to his death from the top of a car park in Manchester whilst trying to escape a car load of queerbashers. Albert was a runaway from a children's home in Salford and was depressed. His short tragic life had been filled with rejection and abuse.

(Albert Kennedy Trust, 2002)

The trust was set up 'so that no lesbian, gay or bisexual young person need feel alone or unwanted', recruiting volunteer carers to provide lesbian or gay homes where homeless teenagers 'can live and rebuild their lives', and volunteer mentors to provide advice and support, for example in applying to college. This is, of course, a voluntary organization responding to situations that arise because of a lack of proactive work by schools and other agencies to counter and address homophobia. Chapter 15 in Reader 2 describes a peer support group for students with same-sex attraction.

The stigma of HIV and AIDS

Children and young people who are HIV positive or who have AIDS are similarly vulnerable to discrimination and exclusionary practice because of the stigma associated with HIV and AIDS, in turn associated with racism and homophobia. The extent and type of ill-health experienced by individuals who are HIV positive are varied and include years free of illness as well as periods when school may be missed. The stigma of HIV and AIDS, though, is linked to the moral panic that has surrounded the 'epidemic' and its links with gay sex. Thus, a social or cultural, as well as medical, phenomenon has been created. In one study of families living with HIV and AIDS, 90 per cent of the young people interviewed talked of having experienced bullying at school (Lewis, 2001). Attitudes have driven many of these young people out of schools through imposed or 'chosen' exclusion.

Reflections on othering

We might have chosen any of the groups included in this unit within this section on othering. Fervent othering, for example, goes on in relation to asylum seekers who are constructed, even by government, as different and undeserving. There is, of course, some kind of othering going on in this unit. We have been conscious of this and keen to focus on the processes at work for particular groups rather than on the groups themselves as problematic. You might like to think about which interventions serve to entrench notions of 'otherness' and which build respect for difference.

6 Doing education differently

For many of the children and young people we have discussed in this unit, schools have either failed or are struggling to include them. The youngsters may experience schooling as demotivating, irrelevant, hostile or inflexible. Their home or personal circumstances may make learning in school extremely difficult and schools' attempts to bridge the gap between their needs and wants and standard provision are too little, too late. Such situations may call for radical alternatives to ordinary schooling.

Notschool

One such radical alternative is Notschool.net:

> ... an online research project looking at ways of re-engaging young people at school age back into learning. These young people have been out of the more traditional educational systems for a variety of personal and logistical reasons.
>
> They include the phobic, ill, disaffected, sick, pregnant and the excluded. Notschool.net is specifically aimed at those for whom traditional alternatives such as home tutoring had not worked.
>
> *(Notschool, 2003)*

The project does everything differently to school. Learning happens largely online where learners (who are called 'researchers') are supported by learning experts. There is a deliberate policy to avoid the language of teacher, pupil, lesson and so on, which may be associated with past failure or bad experiences. People do not have to come together in the same space or at the same time to learn, but do so at their own best times. Learning materials are in 'manageable chunks' that are 'not too linear and not too text based'.

One researcher commented on the scheme:

> I think overall notschool has been good 4 me. Though I don't know how everyone else would find it. I am outgoing (some say loud) with lots of mates so iget socialized outside. But some people might be more isolated than me. Which would make it harder.
>
> Overall though good idea.
>
> Notschool 8–10
>
> Real school 1–10
>
> I no where I d rather be
>
> *(researcher quoted by Notschool, 2003)*

For this young person, the project offers a real alternative to school whilst retaining participation in some kind of structured learning. This raises the question, of course, of why this youngster rated ordinary schooling so poorly, and whether in an inclusive school, in which diversity was valued and systems were more responsive, s/he might not have become disaffected.

Further education

A perhaps less radical alternative to school is further education (FE) college, used more for boys than girls (Osler *et al.*, 2002). FE colleges are increasingly used to provide special or ordinary education courses for under-sixteens who would otherwise be excluded from school or exclude themselves. In Scotland this is sometimes an outcome of a children's hearing. Arrangements may be a formal switch of enrolment or a more informal exclusion by the back door.

Colleges can sometimes offer a fresh start, a different ethos, and a more vocational curriculum. They can have well developed pastoral or guidance systems and well-rehearsed work experience placements. These attributes can re-engage students with education, though there has been little formal evaluation through which we can judge the success of this version of doing education differently.

7 Conclusion

In this unit we have discussed children and young people at the margins of educational life, who are part of the student diversity that inclusive schools need to provide for. In the previous unit we saw some of the proactive, upstream work that is being done to promote the inclusion of these young people. In this unit we have considered some of the downstream, reactive projects that intervene after problems or crises have arisen, sometimes managing to retain young people within the education system. They illustrate some of the exclusionary processes at work in schools that need to be challenged and the structural inequalities and institutionalized discrimination that prevail.

If pupils at the margins are listened to, they tell us that they want to be valued and treated humanely as individuals. They want schools to recognize them and their difference and to challenge bullying and harassment wherever it occurs. If young people have bad school experiences, they can become disaffected and cut off from education. If practice is not inclusive they can be driven out of ordinary provision to become 'someone else's problem'. They can be constructed as other and dehumanized. Re-engagement with education relies on provision that is flexible and tailor-made to meet different needs, interests or circumstances. It often relies upon human relationships and interaction with individuals who are supportive and provide a connection with positive educational experience. While it would be foolish and naïve to rely upon such individualized solutions to societal and systemic problems, we acknowledge that we have a long way to go yet before we no longer need downstream work.

References

Albert Kennedy Trust (2002) 'Background', web page on Albert Kennedy Trust website, www.akt.org.uk/back.htm [accessed June 2002].

Audit Commission (1999) *Missing Out: LEA management of school attendance and exclusion*, London, Audit Commission.

Begum, N. (1994) 'Snow White' in Keith, L. (ed.) *Mustn't Grumble: writing by disabled women*, London, Women's Press.

Blagg, N. (1987), *School Phobia and its Management*, London, Croom Helm.

Blyth, E. and Milner, J. (1987)'Non-attendance and the law: the confused role of social services and education departments' in Reid, K. (ed.) *Combating School Absenteeism*, London, Hodder and Stoughton.

Blyth, E. and Milner, J. (1994) 'Exclusion from school and victim-blaming', *Oxford Review of Education*, 20, pp. 293–306.

Blyth, E. and Milner, J. (1996) *Exclusion from School*, London, Cassell.

Bullock, R. and Little, M. (1994) 'Children's return from state care to school', *Oxford Review of Education*, **20**(3), pp. 307–16.

Bungwe, R. (2002) 'Refugee' in Villiers School (2002) *Migrating Swallows*, London (Southall), Villiers School.

Clarke, L. (2002) 'The most vulnerable of all?', *City Practice*, 4, Spring 2002.

Closs, A. (2000a) 'Absence for medical reasons: a neglected issue in Scottish educational policy', *Scottish Educational Review*, **32**(2), pp. 131–41.

Closs, A. (2000b) 'Introduction to the children and their educational frameworks' in Closs, A. (ed.) *The Education of Children with Medical Conditions*, London, David Fulton.

Closs, A. and Norris, C. (1997) *Outlook Uncertain: enabling the education of children with chronic and/or deteriorating conditions*, Edinburgh, Moray House.

Cullen, M. A., Fletcher-Campbell, F., Bowen, E., Osgood, J. and Kelleher, S. (2000) *Alternative Education Provision at Key Stage 4*, Slough, NFER.

Cullen, M. A., Johnstone, M., Lloyd, G. and Munn, P. (1996) *Exclusion from School and Alternatives; three reports to the Scottish Office*, Edinburgh, Moray House.

Department for Education and Employment (DfEE) (1999a) *Permanent Exclusions from Schools in England 1997/98 and Exclusion Appeals Lodged by Parents in England 1997/98*, Statistical First Release 11/1999, London, DfEE.

Department for Education and Employment (DfEE) (1999b) *Social Inclusion, Pupil Support*, Circular 10/99, London, DfEE.

Department for Education and Employment (DfEE) (2000) *Permanent Exclusions from Schools and Exclusion Appeals, England 1998/99 (provisional)*, Statistical First Release SFR 20/2000, London, DfEE.

Department for Education and Employment and the Department of Health (DfEE/DoH) (2000) *Guidance on the Education of Children and Young People in Public Care*, London, DfEE/DoH.

Department for Education and Skills (DfES) (2002) 'Learning mentor functions' in *Excellence in Cities* website. Available at: http://www.standards.dfes.gov.uk/excellence/policies/Mentors/, (accessed January 2004).

Department for Education and Skills (DfES) (2003a) *Improving Behaviour and Attendance: guidance on exclusion from schools and pupil referral units*, London, DfES.

Department for Education and Skills (DfES) (2003b) *Statistics of Education: permanent exclusions from maintained schools in England*, London, DfES.

Department for Education and Skills (DfES) (2003c) *Statistics of Education: schools in England*, London, DfES.

Department for Education and Skills (DfES) (2003d) 'Welcome to the Access to Education for Children and Young People with Medical Needs website', online, http://www.dfes.gov.uk/sickchildren/ (accessed January 2003).

Department of Education and Science (DES) (1989) *Discipline in Schools. Report of the Commission of Enquiry chaired by Lord Elton*, London, HMSO (the Elton Report).

Fletcher-Campbell, F. and Hall, C. (1990) *Changing Schools? Changing People? The education of children in care*, Slough, NFER.

Flynn, R. (2002) *Short Breaks: providing better access and more choice for Black disabled children and their parents*, Bristol, Policy Press/Joseph Rowntree Foundation.

Ghouri, N. (1999) 'Curb exclusions to tackle homelessness', *Times Educational Supplement*, 2 July.

Gold, K. (1999) 'Children in care failed by councils', *Times Educational Supplement*, 5 March.

Gray, P. and Panter, S. (2000) 'Exclusion or inclusion? A perspective on policy in England for pupils with emotional and behavioural difficulties', *Support for Learning*, **15**(1), pp. 4–7.

Gross, J. and McChrystal, M. (2001) 'The protection of a statement? Permanent exclusions and the SEN Code of Practice', *Educational Psychology in Practice*, **17**(4), pp. 347–59.

Hallam, S. and Castle, F. (2001) 'Exclusion from school: what can help prevent it?' *Educational Review*, **53**(2), pp. 169–79.

Hayden, C. (1997) *Exclusions from Primary Schools*, Buckingham, Open University Press.

Heath, A. F., Colton, M. J. and Aldgate, J. (1994) 'Failure to escape: a longitudinal study of foster children's educational attainment', *British Journal of Social Work*, **24**, pp. 241–60.

Hegarty, K., Lyke, T., Docherty, R. and Douglas, S. (2000) ' "I didn't ask to have this": first-person accounts of young people' in Closs, A. (ed.) *The Education of Children with Medical Conditions*, London, David Fulton.

Howson, J. (1998) 'Bulk of cast-outs are boys', *Times Educational Supplement*, 11 December.

Jackson, S. (1994) 'Educating children in residential and foster care', *Oxford Review of Education*, **20**(3), pp. 267–79.

Jackson, S. and Martin, P. Y. (1998) 'Surviving the care system: education and resilience', *Journal of Adolescence*, **21**, pp. 569–83.

Jordan, E. (1996) 'Education for Travellers' in Befring, E. (ed.) *Teacher Education for Equality*, Association for Teacher Education in Europe 1995 Conference, Oslo, pp. 100–122

Jordan, E. (2001) 'From interdependence, to dependence and independence: home and school learning for Traveller children', *Childhood*, **8**(1), pp. 57–74.

Kurtz, Z. and Thornes, R. (2000) *Health Needs of School Age Children*, London, DfEE and DoH.

Lewis, E. (2001) *Afraid to Say: the needs and views of young people living with HIV/AIDS*, London, National Children's Bureau.

Lloyd, G. and O'Regan, A. (1999) 'Education for social exclusion? Issues to do with the effectiveness of educational provision for young women with "social, emotional and behavioural difficulties"', *Emotional and Behavioural Difficulties*, 4(2), pp. 38–46.

Mallon, B. (1998) *Helping Children Manage Loss; positive strategies for renewal and growth*, London, Jessica Kingsley.

Mental Health Foundation (1999) *The Fundamental Facts*, London, Mental Health Foundation.

Mitchell, L. (1996) 'The effects of waiting time on excluded children' in Blyth, E. and Milner, J. (eds) *Exclusions from School: inter-professional issues for policy and practice*, London, Routledge.

Morris, J. (1998a) *Still Missing? Volume 1: The Experiences of Disabled Children and Young People Living Away from their Families*. London, The Who Cares? Trust.

Morris, J. (1998b) *Still Missing? Volume 2: Disabled children and the Children Act*, London, The Who Cares? Trust.

Munn, P., Lloyd, G. and Cullen, M. A. (2000) *Alternatives to Exclusion from School*, London, Paul Chapman.

Notschool (2003) 'What is Notschool.net?', online at http://www.notschool.net/what/index.html (accessed January 2003).

Office for Standards in Education (Ofsted) (1996) *Exclusions from Secondary Schools*, London, Ofsted.

Office for Standards in Education (Ofsted) (1999) *Special Education 1994–98: a review of special schools, secure units and pupil referral units in England*, London, Ofsted.

Office for Standards in Education (Ofsted) (2000) *Evaluating Educational Inclusion: guidance for inspectors and schools*, London, Ofsted.

The Open University (2001) E242 *Learning for All*, Unit 11/12 *Happy Memories*, Milton Keynes, The Open University.

Osler, A. and Hill, J. (1999) 'Exclusion from school and racial inequality: an examination of government proposals in the light of recent research evidence', *Cambridge Journal of Education*, **29**(1), pp. 33–62.

Osler, A., Street, C., Lall, M. and Vincent, K. (2002) *Not a Problem? Girls and school exclusion*, London, National Children's Bureau and Joseph Rowntree Foundation.

Parsons, C. (1999a) *Education, Exclusion and Citizenship*, London, Routledge.

Parsons, C. (1999b) 'Social inclusion and school improvement', *Support for Learning*, **14**(4), pp. 179–83.

Parsons, C. (2000) *Investigating the Reintegration of Permanently Excluded Young People in England*, Cambridge, INCLUDE.

Quality in Education Centre (1995) *The Truancy File (1): Why truancy matters*, Glasgow, University of Strathclyde/SOEID.

Rathbone CI (1999) *Behaviour Support Plans (BSPs)*, Manchester, Rathbone CI.

Remsbery, N. (2002) 'NCB conference addresses educational rights of refugee children', press release 18 April 2002, online at www.ncb.org.uk [accessed June 2002].

Rhodes, J. and Amjal, Y. (1995) *Solution-Focused Thinking in Schools; behaviour, reading and organization*, London, BT.

Roberts, K. and Harris, J. (2002) *Disabled People in Refugee and Asylum Seeking Communities*, Bristol, The Policy Press/Joseph Rowntree Foundation.

Rutter, J. (2001) *Supporting Refugee Children in Twentieth Century Britain*. Stoke on Trent, Trentham Books.

Searle, C. (2001) *An Exclusive Education: race, class and exclusion in British schools*, London, Lawrence and Wishart.

Shakespeare, T. (1994) 'Cultural representations of disabled people: dustbins for disavowal?' *Disability and Society*, **9**, pp. 283–99.

Sharp, S. and Cowie, H. (1998) *Counselling and Supporting Children in Distress*, London, Sage.

Social Exclusion Unit (1998) *Truancy and School Exclusion*, London, Cabinet Office.

Social Exclusion Unit (2001) *Preventing Social Exclusion*, London, Cabinet Office.

Social Exclusion Unit (2002) *Reducing Re-offending by Ex-prisoners*, London, Cabinet Office.

Stanley, K. (2001) *Cold Comfort: young separated refugees in England*, London, Save the Children.

Tomlinson, S. (1982) *A Sociology of Special Education*, London, Routledge and Kegan Paul.

Vernon, A. (1996) 'A stranger in many camps: the experience of disabled Black and ethnic minority women' in Morris, J. (ed.) *Encounters with Strangers: feminism and disability*, London, Women's Press.

Ward, H. (2001) 'Stories salve scars of war', *Times Educational Supplement* (news section), 12 October 2001, p. 4.

Young Minds (1999) *Response to Government Draft Guidance on Social Inclusion: Pupil Support*, London, Young Minds.

Acknowledgements

Grateful acknowledgement is made to the following for permission to reproduce material in this book.

Unit 9

All photographs are from E243 Video Band B. The Course Team would like to thank the staff and children of Pen Green Centre and Bannockburn High School for their help during the production of Unit 9.

Unit 10

Photographs

Pages 68 and 73: from E243 Video Band C. The Course Team would like to thank the staff and children who contributed to the making of Unit 10.

Text

Pages 79–82: Disability Rights Commission.

Tables

Table 10.1: Hardman, M. and Worthington, J. (2000) 'Educational psychologists' orientation to inclusion and assumptions about children's learning', *Educational Psychology in Practice*, **16**(3), September 2000, Taylor and Francis.

Unit 11

Figures

Figure 11.2: Bradshaw, J. (2000) 'Child poverty and child outcomes', *Children and Society*, **16**.

Illustrations

Page 101: Associated Press; *p. 109*: courtesy of School Councils UK; *p. 114*: Sally and Richard Greenhill.

Unit 12

Illustrations

Page 145: John Birdsall Photography; *p. 149*: Duncan Phillips/Report Digital.

Every effort has been made to contact copyright holders. If any have been inadvertently overlooked the publishers will be pleased to make the necessary arrangements at the first opportunity.